Paycheck 911

Don't Panic . . .

Power Your Job Search!

Joe Turner, "The Job Search Guy"
and Sue Swenson

Paycheck 911

*Copyright 2008
Joseph Turner, Susan Swenson
And Swenson Turner, Inc.*

ISBN-10: #0-9779804-4-8
ISBN-13: #978-0-9779804-4-4

No part of this book may be reproduced or utilized in any form without permission from the publisher.

Excerpts may be quoted for reviews. Inquiries should be made to Swenson Turner Publications.

Published by Swenson Turner Publications
Post Office Box #74454
Phoenix, Arizona 85087-4454
joe@swensonturner.com

Printed in the United States of America

Paycheck 911

Don't Panic . . .

Power Your Job Search!

What they're saying about *Paycheck 911*

"Joe Turner and Sue Swenson have written the definitive book for the realities of today's job market. *Paycheck 911: Don't Panic . . . Power Your Job Search!* offers a system that includes developing your personal brand and researching the hidden job market. You will also learn how to package and market yourself to have an edge on your competition. They cover it all in an easy step-by-step process that any job hunter can follow. A must-read for those who are serious about looking for a great job. Your job future may depend on it."

Molly Mosely
Job Dig
www.jobdig.com

Paycheck 911 -- Table of Contents

WHAT THEY'RE SAYING ABOUT *PAYCHECK 911* 2

INTRODUCTION I
   WHY TRADITIONAL JOB SEARCH METHODS MAY HAVE FAILED YOU I
      You're More on Your Own than Ever I
      Economic Problems on the Horizon; How They Affect You ... II

SECTION I -- FOCUS 1
   DON'T GET TRAPPED IN THE BERMUDA TRIANGLE OF JOB SEARCH 2
      Lack of Focus 2
      Not Understanding the Bigger Picture 3
      Too Much Internet 4
      Summary 5
   THE DIFFERENCE BETWEEN A JOB SEARCH AND JOB HUNTING .. 6
   WHO ARE YOU? 8
      Finding the Real You 8
   FOCUS WITH CAREER ASSESSMENT TESTS 15
      Meyers-Briggs Strong Interest Inventory® 16
      LiveCareer® Career Interest Test 16
      ProjectCareer® Career Aptitude Test 16
      MAPP® (Motivation of Personal Potential) Career Aptitude Test 16
      Princeton Review Career Quiz 17
   YOUR JOB SKILLS INVENTORY WORKSHEET 18

SECTION II -- PACKAGING YOURSELF 27
   JOB HUNTING MEANS *MARKETING YOURSELF* 28
      "Dancing with the Stars"— Seven Job Search Lessons 29
      Summary 31
   FINDING YOUR PERSONAL BRAND 32
      Only Two Types of Employees—Which One Are You? 32
      Know Which Type of Employee You Are 33

To Do	*33*
Summary	*33*
DO YOU KNOW YOUR BRAND IDENTITY?	35
The "Elevator Pitch"	*36*
The USP	*37*
Building Your USP	*37*
Your Personal USP	*40*
YOUR RÉSUMÉ	46
The Four Key Elements Your Résumé MUST Have	*46*
Summary	*53*
A NEW TWIST— THE VIDEO RÉSUMÉ	54
Will It Fly?	*54*
Is a Video Résumé for You?	*55*
A Few Pointers	*55*
Nine Mistakes You Shouldn't Make In Your Video	*56*
Summary	*58*
SECTION III -- RESEARCH	**59**
RESEARCH	60
Finding Jobs, "Hidden" or Posted	*60*
1. Online Job Development Resources	*61*
Web 2.0 and Social Networking Resources	*63*
2. Researching the Hidden Job Market	*70*
DO YOU REALLY WANT TO WORK THERE?	75
Do Your Research First	*75*
Take Ownership of Your Job Search	*77*
Contacting and Following Up with People	*78*
Summary	*78*
Research Tools	*79*
HOW TO USE THE WANT ADS TO FIND POSSIBLE HIDDEN JOBS	91
LIST PROVIDERS–BUYING LISTS	93
SECTION IV -- MARKETING	**97**
MAKING FIRST CONTACT	98
The Letter of Introduction	*98*

How to Develop A Working Relationship With a
Recruiter 104
  Recruiters Can Be Helpful 104
  Dealing Effectively with Human Resources 106
  Are You a "Job Seeker" or a "Job Hunter?" 108
  Phone Presentation 110
  Your Initial Phone Call 112
  The Conversation Itself 113
Shore up Your Network 118
  Network Now 118
  Golden Rule of Networking: "Give Rather than Take" 121
  Summary 124

SECTION V -- INTERVIEWING 125

The Informational Interview 126
  An Old Tool for a New Age: Sue's Story 126
The *Only* Five "Must-Answer" Job Interview Questions
.... 133
  1. "WHY ARE YOU HERE?" 133
  2. "WHAT CAN YOU DO FOR US?" 134
  3. "WILL YOU FIT IN?" 135
  4. "WHAT MAKES YOU UNIQUE?" 135
  5. "HOW MUCH WILL YOU COST US?" 136
Tell Your Stories at the Interview 137
Your Turn: Six Questions You Must *Ask* In Your
Interview 140
  Put It on Paper 142
How to Answer The *Other* Interview Questions 143
  "Tell me about yourself." 143
  "Why do you want to work here?" 144
  "What do you see as your biggest weakness?" 145
Job Search is a Sales Process 149
  The Ten Biggest Interview Killers 149
Post-Interview 152
  Follow up With a Simple Interview "Thank You" Letter ... 152

SECTION VI -- SUPPORT AND RESOURCES 155

DEALING EMOTIONALLY WITH YOUR JOB SEARCH 156
   The Loneliness of the Job Search Process: Sue's Story *156*
   The Five Secrets of Winning Job Hunters *157*
DEALING FINANCIALLY WITH YOUR JOB SEARCH 161
   Did You Lose Your Job? *161*
   Outplacement Services *162*
   Severance Packages *162*
   Separation Benefits *162*
   Ask about References *163*
   Budgeting *163*
   Credit Counseling *163*
   Debt Consolidation Loans *164*
   Tax Deductions for Job Search *164*
   Unemployed and Desperately Seeking a Pay Check? *166*
DEALING SPIRITUALLY WITH YOUR JOB SEARCH 168
   Apply Three Winning Principles from The Secret To Attract
   Your Next Job *169*
   Summary *171*
   Consciousness, Gratitude, and Living in the "Now" *172*
   The Wisdom of It All *173*
ADDITIONAL RESOURCES 174
   Additional Resources for Further Reading *174*
ABOUT THE AUTHORS 175
   Joe's Story *175*
   Sue's Story *175*

Introduction

Why traditional job search methods may have failed you

You may have noticed that job hunting is getting harder every day. In fact, it's probably one of the hardest jobs you'll ever take on. It's stressful, frustrating and scary. And it can seem hopeless.

You're More on Your Own than Ever

Even when your job search runs smoothly, it's still a chore to find gainful employment. To make matters worse, employers structure their hiring process to suit themselves and to serve their bureaucracies. You, the job hunter, don't count. Employers' hiring processes are set up for their convenience and betterment, not yours.

You may often feel like a pariah, a stranger maneuvering in a world that makes no sense, or that you're dealing with a world in which you have no allies. In short, you may think that you've tumbled into the "Alice in Wonderland" environment of the job search world.

Unfortunately, the buck stops with *you*. Don't expect either private sector companies or public agencies to care about you. Their human resource departments are organized to keep you at arm's length. They structure their departments to serve themselves and their corporations. The "don't call us, we'll call you" attitude among these folks is reflected in their whole hiring system.

Don't expect human resource employees to be your friends, either. Their primary goals are to comply with government regulations, push a lot of paper, make themselves look good, and keep their jobs. They have no allegiance to job hunters. In fact, they often take the role of adversary during the hiring process.

Economic Problems on the Horizon; How They Affect You

You're also on your own in a shrinking market. The job search game is getting tougher to play in the U.S. because more people are now competing for fewer jobs due to a weakening economy and continued outsourcing of jobs to other countries.

This tough hiring process has become even tougher because, as a country, we're facing severe economic challenges that affect the job market. For example:

- U.S. debt is now at $9 trillion, causing the dollar to continue losing value relative to other currencies.
- Our trade imbalances are astronomical.
- The housing market and mortgage industries have collapsed and are affecting other industries.
- Oil has climbed to over $130 a barrel at this writing and is predicted to go much higher in the coming months, thus inflating the costs of all goods and services.
- We're in the middle of a war that will cost the U.S. $2.4 trillion or more. Layoffs, housing foreclosures and corporate bankruptcies are escalating, resulting in an economic domino effect that is causing a loss of jobs.

To be successful, you must learn how to distinguish yourself from the crowd, sell value to the employer and uncover 'hidden jobs'.

We wrote *Paycheck 911* to offer you a complete job hunting system that works in today's complex job hiring arena. Our system requires work on your part, and the courage to take a proactive, innovative approach to job search rather than following the traditional job seeking lemmings over the hiring cliff.

Paycheck 911 consists of a five-part, active process to meet the changed demands for successfully finding and landing a job in today's competitive market. This dynamic guide will take you far beyond merely banging out a conventional résumé or CV and using it to apply to jobs that you (and everyone else) have already found on the Web.

And that's not all. As you may have discovered, skills alone don't sell in today's sophisticated market. You deserve more in today's job search arena, and so do the employers to whom you'll be presenting yourself. With this in mind, **here are the five important steps in your new job hunting process:**

Focus

You'll first get focused on who you are and begin to articulate your true skills and abilities.

Packaging Yourself

You'll package yourself by first defining what your major strengths are and the greatest benefits that you bring to your next employer.

Employers read résumés with one question in their minds: "What's in it for me?" So you'll also learn how to translate your skills into benefits that an employer will buy. You'll start by developing a personal brand, one you can articulate easily and that resonates with the employer's needs. You'll separate yourself from your competitors by building a résumé that will sell your achievements and accomplishments and have employers wanting to know more about you.

Research

You'll want to go beyond merely posting your résumé to the job boards and the corporate websites. Since this is what everyone else already does, you'll learn how to separate yourself from the pack and dig deeper to find the names of potential hiring managers and the companies or organizations you should be in front of. Next you'll learn the varied resources you can tap into—some for free and some for a fee—that will lead you to your next step.

Marketing

Once you've learned how to utilize some new resources, you'll have a number of new options. Here, you'll learn effective direct marketing techniques that you can use to widen your search and increase your network. These techniques will enable you to win interviews and leads for jobs and opportunities you would likely never have known about.

Interviewing

The last step is learning how you can successfully sell yourself in the interview by using your personal branding statement and other selling elements that you already implemented in the "Package Yourself" section above.

The goal of *Paycheck 911* is to provide you with a full system for successfully negotiating the waters of today's job market. You'll do this by learning new skills to find and land the job you really want.

If you really want to succeed in a tough job market and learn to do what it takes to win a good job today, then this book is for you.

We wish you a successful job hunt, and the job of your dreams. It's possible to win at the job search game, and *Paycheck 911* is your survival kit to success.

Joe Turner and Sue Swenson
Phoenix, Arizona
June 2008

Section I --
FOCUS

You'll start by becoming focused. In this section, you'll first decide if you're in a career change mode or a job search mode. Once that's established, you'll start developing your all-important Personal Brand. Here is where you'll develop a Unique Selling Proposition for yourself that will be the very foundation on which your entire job hunt will rest.

Don't Get Trapped In the Bermuda Triangle Of Job Search

Navigating today's rocky seas of job search can feel as treacherous as being caught in a raging storm in the Bermuda Triangle. If you can't avoid these three major pitfalls, your job search will sink into an abyss.

Lack of Focus

The first step in a successful job search begins with identifying your goals. Clarify specifically what you want in your next job or career. This includes identifying your next job title. I've heard countless job seekers say, "I'll take anything" or "I'm open", when asked what kind of job they're seeking. The candidate who'll take anything ends up with *nothing*.

Look at your résumé, for starters. What is your objective? Many job seekers either fail to state their objective, or they list several objectives. Either extreme can work against you; you'll appear unfocused, uncommitted or unqualified.

Gaining clarity will lead to identification of your next job or career. If you're having trouble focusing, look online for help; you can find many free career assessment tests. Or, seek the services of a career coach. These professionals specialize in helping people to identify their goals, passions, life's purpose and transferable skills.

Check the ***Career Change Resources*** section at the end of this book for further resources on assessment testing and career coaching. Be sure to screen career coaches with your own list of questions about their experience, fees, coaching methods, etc.

Not Understanding the Bigger Picture

Avoid focusing on your own needs. When you're clear on what type of job or career to pursue, your next step is to understand how to market yourself competitively. You bring to a potential employer a unique set of work experience, skills, aptitudes, abilities and personality traits. Yet none of these assets has any meaning unless you understand that your focus must now shift to the employer.

Imagine yourself seated in the hiring manager's chair. Role-play as both the applicant and the hiring manager. What does the hiring manager want to know about you? What message does that individual want to hear from you? What is this person looking for in an employee?

We wrote *Paycheck 911* to help you package your work experience, transferable skills and other assets into a consistent, winning message that answers the hiring manager's critical question, "If I hire you, what's in it for me?" You'll be able to communicate your USP (Unique Selling Proposition); that is, your value to the employer as a potential employee who can either make money or save money for the company.

As you understand the bigger picture of a corporate balance sheet, you can more easily sell yourself as a potential asset to any company. One of the exercises in this book will direct you to make a comprehensive list of your activities and responsibilities. You'll see which ones help to save money, make money or save time for the company. Once you start thinking in this manner, you can more easily develop several examples to use. And once you have several examples, you'll be able to incorporate them into your "complete package" and begin marketing yourself more successfully.

You'll develop a better résumé, plus you'll perform better in your phone screens and interviews because you'll be talking about the benefits you can bring to your employer. Once you begin marketing yourself in this new way, you'll notice a difference in your results. You'll also steer clear of a major obstacle that's capsizing many of your competitors.

Too Much Internet
Avoid hitting job search icebergs

Most job searchers post their résumés on Monster®, Yahoo®, LinkedIn® and even Facebook® these days. The trouble is, so does everyone else. Unfortunately, this represents only about 20% of the actual hires being made.

Like an iceberg, where the majority of the ice is hidden under the surface of the water, it's estimated that 80% of job opportunities are likewise "hidden." Even with the advent of the Internet, only small fractions of all available jobs are advertised. When you limit yourself to the 20% of total advertised and accessible job openings, you sacrifice your job prospects to the whims of the open marketplace. You increase your competition for those jobs because everyone else has access to those same publicly listed opportunities. Only when you decide to separate yourself from the pack will you increase your chances of being hired.

To begin with, there are fewer applicants for these hidden jobs. You also maximize your chances of getting a better quality job, because often the best job opportunities are quietly passed along by word of mouth and are never advertised to the general public.

Researching the hidden job market is hard work. You'll need to network with as many friends, colleagues and family members as you can. You'll also need information from sources that range from the Internet to your local library. For example, begin looking into social networking sites for names of people you might contact. Go beyond the herd to develop a list of companies you'd like to work for. Your local library has great resources, too, including Hoovers®, EBSCO®, and ReferenceUSA®, to name a few that are free. Check out LinkedIn®, Spoke® and ZoomInfo® for names of people who work at these companies.

There are also list providers. These are vendors who specialize in providing data for the direct marketing industry. This data includes names of businesses throughout the world as well as names and titles of managers who work there. Once located, you can contact these people and introduce yourself. When you can talk in terms of the benefits you bring to an employer, you separate yourself from your competitors. You'll also get better leads and more interviews when you begin navigating the uncharted waters of the hidden job market.

Summary

You can avoid the three major pitfalls that can sink most job searches by:

- Sharpening your focus
- Talking about the benefits you bring to an employer
- Moving beyond the Internet to look for unadvertised jobs.

As we move forward from here, you'll be growing from a passive job *searcher* to a more active job *hunter*.

It won't necessarily be an easy job, but if you put these three actions together, you'll have more control during your job hunt journey. You'll also avoid the three major obstacles that doom most job searchers today.

The Difference Between A Job Search and Job Hunting

Most job searches end badly (either no job or compromising with a lesser job), not because there was some "secret ingredient" that most people missed. Rather, it was the expectation that a job search was supposed to be an easy, hands-off, remote "Internet" sort of experience, as if it were something like ordering your next job from Amazon.com®.

While it's true that technology has greatly "enhanced" (some would say mucked up) the typical job search experience today, it remains a passive and ineffective way to conduct a job search. It's partly the fault of employers and their bureaucratic HR departments—operations that wall themselves off from the hordes of job seekers so that *no contact* can be made. But most job seekers have fallen prey to the siren call of the easy, "point & click," no-muss-no-fuss job search approach.

This ineffective scheme entails developing a conventional résumé that attempts to sell skills, then blasting it everywhere imaginable—to job sites like Monster®, Careerbuilder®, HotJobs®, CraigsList®, and many others. Add to this the enormous number of faceless recruiting firms, then top it off by applying directly to any corporate site's appropriate *job posting du jour*—then sit back and wait.

This is today's typical job search model. It almost never works. How will you know it isn't working for you? The phone won't ring, and when that happens, panic will set in and you'll begin to scramble.

While the old way may seem neat and clean even though not terribly effective, it's becoming *even less so* as the economic situation declines.

The major problem is that typical job searching has progressively degenerated into a passive, ineffective Internet-based activity. This might work well for ordering items online, but as a process, it fails for job search. Why? Because there's an inherent inconsistency in the process itself. Job search always has been and always will be a very human, high-touch process, but today's technology has stuffed it into an electronic, hands-off medium. It isn't working well this way because the basic elements of a successful search have always remained the same—and simply aren't built into the "technology solution."

Job searching must include:
- An effective method to sell the benefits that employers recognize and want.
- Developing a *conversation* with an actual decision-maker.

Make no mistake, an effective job search requires that you get your hands dirty and your whole body and soul involved. You'll need to rethink who you are and what you bring to the table in new ways you've probably not recognized or considered before. You'll also need to develop ways to put yourself in front of people with whom you *can* have a conversation and then know what to say and how to say it.

Most likely, you'll be challenged in this newer, non-passive and more direct approach to your search. In short, you'll become a **Job Hunter** looking for your prey. You'll take your rightful power position and stop passively waiting by the phone or quivering from the wrath of some unseen HR staffer should you call to inquire about the status of your résumé.

So, let's get our hands dirty.

Who Are You?

Finding the Real You

Packaging yourself requires knowing your biggest strengths and talents. If you've worked long enough, you likely have a good idea about what some of your strengths are. Your strengths in large part fuel your accomplishments in your work.

Here are two examples of well-written résumés; read them now so you'll have a rough idea of a couple of models. We'll bring you back to them later, when you're ready to structure your own "sales presentation."

SAMIR VENKAT

17790 Windsong Terrace •Falls Church, Virginia 21427

(H) 703-555-2780 • (C) 703-555-3467 •

name@domain.com

OBJECTIVE

Director Software Engineering/Information Technology

SUMMARY

Seasoned Director of Software Engineering whose strength in planning and execution of large Web-based solutions in Healthcare & Telecom industries has saved my previous two employers $23M in development costs.

KEY SKILLS

Project Management • Team Leadership • Client Relations • Resource Allocation • Strategic Planning Prototype Design • Budget Management • Requirement Analysis • Test & Validate • Product Management

Information technology, software development, research, development, problem-solving/decision making, leadership, oral/written communications, team-building, performance and productivity improvement, results-driven, technical research, analysis, planning, management, motivate, mentor.

TECHNICAL EXPERTISE

OS: Windows 2000/XP/2003, Linux, UNIX

PROGRAMMING: J2EE, JMS, JCA, JNI, JDO, Jaxb, Javascript, Swing, Applet, ASP.NET, COM+, SQL, HTML, XML, SOAP, C/C++, VC++, IPC, RPC, Shell Scripts

DATABASES: MS-SQL, MYSQL, ODBC/JDBC, Oracle, PL/SQL

PROTOCOLS: HL7, DICOM, TCP/IP, HTTP, SOAP, ATM, RSVP, GMPLS, OSPF, SIP, SNMP

OTHER : Websphere, Jbuilder, Visual Studio, UML, Rational Rose, Clearcase, Source GearVault, Dragnet, MS Project, Soarian Clinicals, Siemens Servo Ventilator, BBraun IVpump, DataCaptor

PROFESSIONAL EXPERIENCE

NOVACHECK, INC.—2006 - Present

Director—Software Engineering ~ *ASP.NET, ORACLE 10G, SQLSERVER, HL7* ~

Responsible for managing & deploying Patient Safety Reporting Solution in Healthcare facilities.

ACHIEVEMENTS & RESULTS

• Built, trained & directed strong team of developers & managers in short period & delivered quality product on time.

• Rescued poorly managed outsourced project and built in-house development team that cut development costs down by $1M (50%).

• Reduced development costs by $600K through reduction in re-work & bugs, improved customer satisfaction and increased productivity by advocating Agile Software process.

• Eliminated errors and minimized the time required for software builds, installations and upgrades by creatively architecting Build/Release plan & Configuration Management plan resulting in a savings of over $30K.

OTHER DUTIES

• Improved quality of software using techniques like Refactoring, unit test-frameworks, design-patterns.

• Designed defect-tracking process and deployed a defect-tracking tool to maintain the defects & enhancements linked with the versioned code-changes.

GE MEDICAL SYSTEMS—2001 - 2006

Program Architect ~ *COM+, J2EE, SQLSERVER, HL7, DICOM* ~

Architected integration of Departmental Systems like Oncology, Radiology, ORMS, Pharmacy, Critical Care Systems with the enterprise Healthcare Information System (Soarian).

ACHIEVEMENTS & RESULTS

• Championed & advocated Agile Software process that minimized delays, achieved quick feedback software cycles, and gained productivity & customer satisfaction.

Reduced development time by 3 months ($500K) by advocating Agile Software process with the development teams located overseas, and increased productivity by minimizing misdirection and communication latencies.

• Architected & implemented integration of systems effectively, minimized on-site integration time, saving $200K in travel costs for the teams located overseas.

• Identified and developed solutions to eliminate performance bottle-necks in the system, improving the quality of the product resulting in $40K in savings in additional hardware that would be required otherwise. This also reduced the cost of the product providing increased sales.

OTHER DUTIES

• Architected the integration of Siemens Pharmacy system with Siemens' Enterprise Healthcare Information system; provided design & performance support; coordinated project with satellite teams.

• Investigated use of RFID in the Healthcare system; prototyped a solution, & demonstrated it to senior management. This resulted in adding new feature & product line in the Siemens Healthcare system.

CISCO SYSTEMS—2000 - 2001

Lead Software Engineer ~ *TCP/IP, SS7, ATM, BACKHAUL, RUDP, RSVP* ~ Led the development of Telecom & Datacom signaling delivery protocols to control circuit-switching & packet-switching equipment while bridging heterogeneous networks.

• Led dual-Ethernet development to provide IP redundancy to control SS7 signal link terminator device.

• Designed, implemented, & maintained components of VSC3000 application; provided call management, including telephony switching, protocol termination, & protocol translation for media gateways.

• Devised & created test plans to perform signaling for ISDN-PRI over the IP network.

• Actively aided in the ISO-9001 / GEM certification process.

KFORCE CONSULTING, INC.—1997 - 2000

Senior Technical Consultant ~ *C++, JAVA, TCP/IP, RSVP, SIP, ATM, OSPF, SNMP* ~

Paycheck 911

Provided technical & consulting services, developing telecommunication & Web-based applications for clients like SPRINT, Sabre Group, & MCI-WorldCom.

- Designed & implemented an application integrated with SIP / RSVP / COPS protocols for Internet telephony & guaranteed QOS over the IP network.

- Redesigned & implemented a communication layer for a reservation bandwidth server application in a multi-threaded environment to create and manage reserved bandwidth network connections.

- Implemented a Web interface to interface with a back-end legacy system to process booking air ticket through the Internet.

- Designed Multi-vendor ATM Provisioning System (MAPS), implemented its interfaces with Nortel / NEC's ATM switches / EMS, providing PVC's over the network & routing IP / FrameRelay traffic over the ATM backbone.

- Developed ATM adaptation logical trunk connections for signaling virtual channels (SVC).

GLOBAL INTERNET—1996
Network Engineer

Provide troubleshooting & operational support to customers.

- Performed network monitoring & solved problems associated with IP Connectivity.

- Configured CISCO Routers, Firewalls, DNS, Newsfeed, & mail service.

EDUCATION, TRAINING, CERTIFICATIONS

MS Comp Science, University of Arizona, Tuscon, AZ, 1996

BS Mech Engg, MS Ramaiah Inst of Tech, Bangalore, India, 1990

Advanced courses in networking, software economics, & GMU, VA, UML, J2EE, COM+, DICOM, Siemens' OPENLink, HL7 Certification, QMS, Agile Software Development, Scrum Master Certification

PERSONAL

Green card holder

Starting on the following page is another résumé sample that provides a good model that you can return to later as an example of good form and excellent content.

Paycheck 911

Ed Cavallo
Project Manager

18 Kessman Court, El Dorado Hills, CA 95760
916-555-8244
name@domain.com

SUMMARY
Seasoned project manager whose strengths in strategic market focus, revenue enhancement, and team development have saved my employer over $500k while completing over $5 million worth of projects during the past 3 years.

CORE COMPETENCIES
Project management • Coaching • Operations • Sales • Marketing • **Decision Making** • Team **Leadership** • Team Building • Customer Service • Prioritize Tasks with Competing Deadlines • Attention to Detail • Implementing Solutions • Building Relationships • **Problem-Solving** • **Oral/Written Communications** • **Performance & Productivity Improvement** • Meet Deadlines • Manage Competing Priorities • Mentor Skills • Planning Strategies • Analyzing Problems • Budgeting • Leadership/management • Branch management • Development Action Planning • Creating an Inclusive Environment • Organizational Skills Customer Relations • Investment Consulting • Business Portfolio Management • Experienced Scheduler • Operations Management • MS Word • Excel • PowerPoint • Outlook • People Soft • Calendaring Programs Internet Communications • Internet Researching

ACHIEVEMENTS & RESULTS

Improved revenues in 2 under-performing branches exceeding goals by 76% every quarter for 2 years by analyzing financial data (expenses, operating costs, profit/loss) and implementing specific action plans.

Hired and trained a new team that increased sales volume by 122% within 15 months.

Reduced turnover by 65% over previous management within 15 months through my mentor program and development plans.

Trained 15 new sales people to help **transform 2 failing branches** into the top-producing sales team in Central California.

My program **saved the bank $215K in training expenses** and reduced project completion times as the personnel gained experience.

Won the Leadership, Excellence, and Dedication award in 2007 for outstanding achievements during my management role.

Achieved Number-One Sales for opening 425 self-directed brokerage accounts in 1 year by networking with clients, mailing correspondence, cross-selling, and working with business partners.

Exceeded sales goals every quarter as much as 190% and received the highest customer service scores in the Monterey Bay market as a result of my training program.

Increased our customer satisfaction survey scores by 30% on average by coaching my team on the proper way to provide a great customer experience.

Reached 410% of goal for self directed brokerage accounts which raised profit 27% alone by building alliances with strategic partners and nurturing a solid system for co-selling and co-marketing efforts.

PROFESSIONAL EXPERIENCE

Chase Bank
Branch Manager 8/2006 - 1/2008
Managed 2 branches financial analysis, operations, client investment portfolios, staffing, Human Resource duties, sales, and audit projects where I delegated project tasks to teams. $10 Million in sales annually and employed 19 people. These branches brought in 15% of my district's revenue.

Premier Client Manager 11/2004 - 8/2006
Managed client investment portfolios, financial analysis, sales, staffing, budget, and operations

Alto Ristorante
Customer Service Manager 10/2000 - 6/2004
Managed marketing efforts, customer service, sales, staffing, scheduling, training, payroll, budget, and operations for this $5 Million restaurant with 30-40 employees.

Via Sorrento Association
Customer Service Manager 6/1996 - 6/1999
Managed facilities, operations, training, staffing, and customer service for this $20 Million golf association of 35 employees.

EDUCATION
B.A., Business Management, 2005, University of California Santa Cruz

PROFESSIONAL AFFILIATIONS, MEMBERSHIPS
NASD/SEC series 7 and 66

Paycheck 911

We will return to these two résumés later on because they each contain vital elements for successful integration into both human-centered and electronic résumé entry systems. We will cover each facet separately in the pages ahead.

Focus with Career Assessment Tests

If you're not sure of your core strengths, or if you'd like to verify the strengths you believe you have, consider taking a career aptitude assessment test or survey.

This sort of assessment is most often used to narrow down possible career choices and open the door to new possibilities. For your purposes, the key objective of such a test would be to help you understand yourself better and to capitalize on the strengths you already have. You'll also be able to better verbalize those strengths in the *Unique Selling Proposition* you'll develop for yourself in the next chapter.

There are a number of free tests you can take on the Internet. Some are free, quick and convenient; each one will yield a decent degree of accuracy. In some cases, with an investment of only about 20 minutes of your time, you can produce focused insights into your skills and abilities, PLUS receive lists of specific jobs or industries you might want to explore.

These tests use a series of questions about your interests, style of working, and how you interact with others. Your answers can help you figure out your natural preferences and strengths.

On our "Job Search Guy" site (www.jobchangesecrets.com), you can link to the LiveCareer® Assessment test for no charge and get your results in about 20 minutes. You'll find out your interests, work preferences and work personality. Here is the direct link:

http://www.interview444.com/Career.html

There are a number of other career and aptitude assessment tests available on the Web. You'll find that some are free at the initial level and will involve costs for more advanced versions or enhanced information, but the initial, no-cost version may be all you need in order to get most of what you need to identify your basic core aptitudes (things you're good at). If you feel like exploring more about yourself or you're also considering a possible career change, here is a sampling of possibilities:

Meyers-Briggs Strong Interest Inventory®

http://www.personalitydesk.com/career-tests.php

One of the most respected names in personality testing, this measures your unique interest profile and compares it to profiles for hundreds of careers. You'll receive a 19-page report that includes a detailed interest profile, extensive career rankings, and a personalized action plan for career development. There is a cost for this test.

LiveCareer® Career Interest Test

http://www.livecareer.com/click/track.asp?ref=1255

A free aptitude test that will help you identify your own unique qualities and match them to careers that you may find rewarding. This aptitude test can help you determine your interests, work preferences and work personality.

ProjectCareer® Career Aptitude Test

http://www.projectcareer.com/?code=PF1-

Free aptitude test. Other free assessment tests are also offered at this link: http://www.careerexplorer.net/aptitude.asp

MAPP® (Motivation of Personal Potential) Career Aptitude Test

http://www.assessment.com

Free assessment and with sample report and five free job matches.

Princeton Review Career Quiz

http://www.princetonreview.com/cte/quiz/career_quiz1.asp

Identifies your career interests and work style. Also identifies careers that are good matches.

It is good to review the possibilities above, but in the next chapter you will complete a job skills survey to discern your top six skill areas and the resulting action for each one. This will be important, because you'll then be able to build your Unique Selling Proposition—or Brand Identity.

Your Job Skills Inventory Worksheet

If you've taken one or more of the aptitude assessment tests above, you already have a good idea where your main strengths lie. If not, or if you don't want to take the time right now to do that, complete the Job Skills Inventory Worksheet that appears below. You'll use this information when you develop your important *branding statement* in the next chapter. First, check all the items that you believe apply to you.

Job Skills Inventory Worksheet – Soft Skills

☐	Analyzing	☐	Arranging
☐	Assessing performance	☐	Assessing progress
☐	Assessing quality	☐	Assisting
☐	Attending to detail	☐	Auditing
☐	Budgeting	☐	Building co-operation
☐	Building credibility	☐	Building relationships
☐	Building structures	☐	Calculating
☐	Classifying	☐	Client relations
☐	Coaching	☐	Communicating feelings
☐	Communicating ideas	☐	Communicating (written)
☐	Communicating instructions	☐	Communicating (nonverbal)
☐	Communicating (verbal)	☐	Computer literacy
☐	Conceptualizing	☐	Consulting
☐	Coordinating	☐	Correcting

Paycheck 911

- ☐ Corresponding
- ☐ Customer service
- ☐ Data entry
- ☐ Decision-making
- ☐ Delegating
- ☐ Developing designs
- ☐ Developing talent
- ☐ Directing
- ☐ Drawing
- ☐ Editing
- ☐ Empathizing
- ☐ Engineering
- ☐ Facilitating
- ☐ Financial planning
- ☐ Formulating
- ☐ Healing
- ☐ Imagining
- ☐ Influencing
- ☐ Intervening
- ☐ Inventing
- ☐ Leading people
- ☐ Lifting
- ☐ Managing tasks

- ☐ Counseling
- ☐ Data analysis
- ☐ Data processing
- ☐ Decorating
- ☐ Designing
- ☐ Developing systems
- ☐ Diagnosing
- ☐ Drafting
- ☐ Driving
- ☐ Educating
- ☐ Enforcing
- ☐ Evaluating
- ☐ Filing
- ☐ Forecasting
- ☐ Fund raising
- ☐ Helping others
- ☐ Implementing
- ☐ Initiating
- ☐ Intuiting
- ☐ Investigating
- ☐ Lecturing
- ☐ Listening
- ☐ Marketing

Paycheck 911

- ☐ Marketing communications
- ☐ Multitasking
- ☐ Nurturing
- ☐ Organizing
- ☐ Persuading
- ☐ Program managing
- ☐ Project Managing
- ☐ Public speaking
- ☐ Recording
- ☐ Reporting
- ☐ Selling and marketing
- ☐ Servicing
- ☐ Supervising
- ☐ Teaching
- ☐ Team leading
- ☐ Tending
- ☐ Tooling
- ☐ Troubleshooting
- ☐ Writing

- ☐ Motivating
- ☐ Negotiating
- ☐ Observing
- ☐ Performing
- ☐ Prescribing
- ☐ Programing computers
- ☐ Promoting
- ☐ Reconstructing
- ☐ Repairing
- ☐ Researching
- ☐ Selling
- ☐ Servicing customers
- ☐ Surveying
- ☐ Team building
- ☐ Telephone skills
- ☐ Testing
- ☐ Training
- ☐ Using equipment

Add other possible choices to your list

☐		☐	
☐		☐	
☐		☐	

Now that you've selected all the skills you believe you have to offer a new employer, the next task is to *prioritize* the skills you checked off on the Job Skills Inventory Worksheet to determine your top six (6) soft skills. Go back to the previous exercise and give each item a rank order.

List Your Top Six Skills Here in Priority Order	
Skill #1	
Skill #2	
Skill #3	
Skill #4	
Skill #5	
Skill #6	

Next, take each skill above and relate it to a specific action or result. Try to define each action as an activity that directly benefits the employer.

Example: Suppose you checked "organizing" as a top skill. As a result of this skill, *you were able to rewrite your administrative office's "Standard Office Procedural" document that included a more streamlined approach to running the day-to-day office functions.*

Example: Suppose you checked "negotiating" as a top skill. As a result of this skill, *you were able to engage in extended conversations with a prospect and arrive at an agreeable selling price of the product you sold that resulted in a successful sale as well as a profit for your employer.*

Proven Outcomes from Each Top Skill
Skill #1 resulted in this action or outcome:
Skill #2 resulted in this action or outcome:
Skill #3 resulted in this action or outcome:
Skill #4 resulted in this action or outcome:
Skill #5 resulted in this action or outcome:
Skill #6 resulted in this action or outcome:

You now have your top skills and their corresponding actions. The next task is to assign employer-oriented benefits to each of the six top-priority outcomes above.

Using the spaces below, quantify—*in terms of benefits to your employer*—the results you have been able to obtain.

For your highest priority skill above and its resultant action:

1. What was the biggest or most important role, duty or project that you performed or were involved in?

And what quantifiable benefits to your employer resulted from your involvement?

Now, combine each of the statements and benefits above so that they read as a complete sentence. ***Here's an Example:***

Duty or Role:

Managing benefits, STD, LTD, Life, Medical Dental, 401K

Benefit:

Saved company $113,566 by switching to more cost-effective programs. Staying with the previous insurance companies would have increased our rates by 18%.

Combined Role and Benefit = Achievement Sentence:

Saved company $113,566 by switching to more cost-effective programs to manage benefits, STD, LTD, Life, Medical Dental, 401K. Staying with the previous insurance companies would have increased our rates by 18%.

(On the résumé, this would become a bullet statement that might read: ***Saved my employer more than $113,500 from 2005 to the present by***

Paycheck 911

researching and implementing alternate programs to manage Benefits, STD, LTD, Life, Medical Dental, 401K. Staying with the previous insurance companies would have increased our rates by 18%.)

Now compare this with the original statement, which was: **Manage Benefits, STD, LTD, Life, Medical Dental, 401K.**

Can you see the difference? Your readers will, especially when you have included several powerful benefit statements like this. This may take some thought, so put some time into it. Use the space below.

Later, when you have more time, repeat this exercise for other important or meaningful roles, duties or projects you performed for all of your employers. Not only is it good practice in calculating and expressing *results*, but you may surprise yourself with just how much impact you have had on the jobs you have done and the companies you have worked for throughout your career.

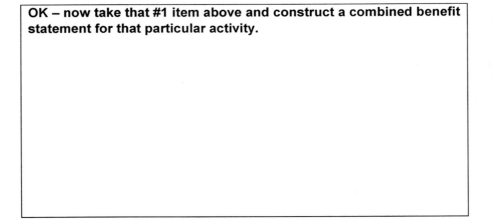

OK – now take that #1 item above and construct a combined benefit statement for that particular activity.

Use the format on the following page to outline and quantify the results you achieved in the other roles, duties or projects you prioritized earlier.

Paycheck 911

What was another important role, duty or project that you performed or were involved in?

And what quantifiable benefits to your employer resulted from your involvement?

OK – now construct a combined benefit statement for that particular activity.

Duplicate this page as many times as needed to develop new skill-application-quantified outcome statements.

Section II --
PACKAGING YOURSELF

In this section you will develop a Brand Identity and Unique Selling Propositions for yourself—vital first steps toward a "marketing approach" for your job hunt—and you will also begin to evolve the résumé items that will bring you to the attention of potential employers by setting you apart from and above all other competitors.

Job Hunting Means
Marketing Yourself

Marketing can be defined in the simplest of terms as "the process of finding buyer(s) for your product or service." Corporations willingly spend billions of dollars each year in their efforts to attract and qualify customers who will spend trillions to purchase their products and services. They do this because marketing works.

Your job hunt requires a similar "systems approach" to marketing yourself. This means that every piece of correspondence and verbal contact including e-mail messages, telephone calls, letters of inquiry, résumés and thank you notes must have a consistent message that will sell you as an asset to your prospective employer.

While you may not be willing or able to spend a fortune, plan to invest a certain percentage of your time and money to find one or more qualified buyers of your talents. Finding a qualified buyer means more than just posting your résumé on the Web. Like a national advertiser, you must widen your scope and include a number of new avenues in your approach.

To post résumés only on the Internet would be like Toyota selling cars by advertising only on TV. There is hardly a place you can go today that you won't run into the name Toyota—print ads in magazines and newspapers, brochures and other sales collateral, banner, flash and video ads on the Web, ads on dedicated websites, ads on affiliate websites, ads camouflaged as consumer information, sponsorships in marathon races, charity events, auto-related websites, and now even good ol' boy NASCAR has recently begun running Toyotas. A few years ago, many of these avenues didn't even exist.

So widen your perspective. Read on. We'll show you how to add several new (and perhaps nontraditional) elements to your job search that will raise you above your growing competition so you'll be noticed—and hired!

"Dancing with the Stars"— Seven Job Search Lessons

As a starter, consider a popular TV show called "Dancing with the Stars." It's a great metaphor for seven very important traits that will serve you well as you learn more and work harder to get a good job.

Perhaps, like many others, you've been riveted by this wildly popular TV program that pairs celebrities with professional dancers glammed up in sequined costumes, makeup and dazzling hairdos. Each week, the couples compete through slickly choreographed dances such as the cha-cha, waltz and tango as they overcome obstacles and strive for high scores from the judges—plus votes from the public to advance to the next round of competition. Actually, it's a classic "hero's journey" on the dance floor, demonstrating seven very practical lessons that job seekers can identify with on many levels.

Here they are:

1. **Believe in Yourself** – To win, the dancers must believe in themselves. Sure, they might be celebrities, but none of them has ever danced competitively. As we watch each week, we witness them evolve from self-doubt and frustration to poise and self-confidence. The job search journey has a built-in growth mechanism. It nudges the job seeker, through challenges, into a stronger sense of self. As the old adage says, "What doesn't kill you makes you stronger."

2. **Turn Criticism into Welcome Feedback** – Dozens of hours of hard work go toward preparing for each dance. No matter. After their live performance, we'll witness many of the dancers receive some rather harsh criticism. While some may argue and get defensive, the more successful dancers will apply these comments to their next week's dance routine. These couples make every effort to accept feedback from the judges as a gift for improvement while those who argue are more quickly

voted off. Feedback from prospective employers and hiring managers is vital to your search process too. Getting defensive and feeling victimized only prolongs the job search. Learning from your errors is the mark of maturity, and enables you to win your next job.

3. **Maintain a Winner's Focus** – The winning dancers learn to focus. This is one of the biggest issues between the professional dancers and their partners. As the celebrities master focusing, their dancing improves. This is true for job seekers as well. It's impossible to achieve a job search goal if you don't clarify what you want. Without focusing and becoming crystal clear about your goal, your roadmap is confusing and you wander in circles.

4. **Work Hard, and then Even Harder** – These dancers work harder than they ever dreamed they would, just to keep up with their competitors. They keep raising the bar for each other. A successful job seeker must be committed to hard work. Finding the right job is often much harder than doing the actual job once you're hired. No matter how hard the search seems, apply yourself even more. Keep going that extra mile.

5. **Develop a Winning Attitude** – After four seasons, no dancer has ever won "Dancing with the Stars" with a bad attitude. And so it is with your job search. It's critical to view yourself as an empowered person. You're not a victim. You know that rejection and setbacks are temporary and not personal. They are part of the process. You know that ultimately you're going to win this challenge. You focus on positive thoughts and outcomes. You don't accept defeat. You aren't attached to the outcome of any particular set of interviews. You need to know that when you don't get offered a particular job, it simply means that there's a better one up ahead for you.

6. **Market and Sell Yourself to Success** – The celebrities and professional dancers understand that while in front of the camera, they are continuously marketing and selling themselves to the judges and the viewing public. Everything they do and say is a statement and a message about who they are. And so it is with your job search. Every telephone call, e-mail note, letter, card, and piece of information that you send out, including your résumé, must represent you well. It must be consistent and present you in your best light, with a focus on the needs of the employer rather than you.

7. **Recognize That People Love Winners** – There are differences among the dancers. Some show enthusiasm, and some express varying degrees of negativity. As the competition progresses, the enthusiastic dancers win over the judges and the audience. Enthusiasm is contagious. People who have learned to see themselves as winners project this image to their audience. Potential employers will often hire less experienced applicants who exude enthusiasm and high energy over more experienced applicants who seem lukewarm about the job.

Summary

"Dancing with the Stars" is a good metaphor for today's job search experience. Both involve a long process full of obstacles, setbacks and rejection, and both endeavors require a similar winning formula for success. Taking the metaphor further, you're now ready to take some of your "dance steps" such as your new branding statement, and you'll put them to music as you move further into this process and actually start to make contact with real people who can help move you toward that "perfect job."

Finding Your Personal Brand

Only Two Types of Employees—Which One Are You?

Companies are in business to make money or they do not survive. Even government agencies and non-profit organizations must survive on limited tax revenues, grant monies, bequests, or contributions.

That means all employees are accountable to the bottom line. Whether your job is to:

- Answer the phones
- Provide customer support
- Direct offshore manufacturing
- Write software code
- Drive a truck
- Train new employees
- Balance the books
- Test the products
- Write the PR
- Manage the team/group/division . . .

Whatever you do, it all boils down to only two areas insofar as management is concerned. You must be either:

1. *Helping to make money for your company, or*
2. *Helping to save money for your company.*

Perhaps your job may involve *saving time* for others in the company. If this is the case, then you *save money* so the company can invest to make more money elsewhere. (Example: administrative assistants who routinely run interference for their bosses, sparing them mundane minutiae each day, saving their company money.)

Here is the bottom line:

Know Which Type of Employee You Are

You need to think, "How would hiring me help the company make or save money?" Said another way, "Companies want to spend money on *solutions to problems.*" They don't hire people to be liabilities on their balance sheet; they want their people to be *assets*. This means that you must present yourself as a *money-maker/money-saver* and a *problem solver*.

To Do

First, look for opportunities that demonstrate how you have been a problem solver. Start by looking for occurrences in the past when you either:

- Made money for the company
- Saved money for the company
- Saved time—and hence saved money—for the company

Here's an example of the first point:

Bill functions as a lead generation specialist for the marketing department. His role is to use specialized software to research lists of names to deduce which few are the best prospects for future marketing programs the company undertakes. Bill makes money for his company. Although he doesn't actually make the sale, each lead he generates is worth a dollar value since one out of every 20 of these leads will produce a sale.

Second, make a list of your own examples. Then take the best two or three and hone each one down to a story you can tell.

And *third*, practice verbally so you can discuss each example as a story of about 30 to 60 seconds, off the cuff and without notes. You'll be using these stories when you interview.

Summary

Once you understand the basic concept of how you fit into the balance sheet and in the bigger picture for your employer, you'll be ready to take the next important step of separating yourself from the masses by developing your *Unique Selling Proposition* or *Branding Statement.*

Do You Know Your Brand Identity?

You've already discovered what type of employee you are from the exercises that you've done so far. Now you need to develop an effective way to communicate who you are to a wider audience.

It's imperative to have more than just keywords on your résumé. To get noticed and to be taken seriously today, you must quickly distinguish yourself from all other candidates for the job you want; you need to generate *specific interest in you* on the part of people you've probably never met. Not an easy task!

If you want some good insight into how to do that these days, walk up and down the aisles of any grocery store. As you traverse the cereal aisle, for instance, you'll see dozens of products that have fought for shelf space and are now fighting for your attention and asking you to purchase them.

- **Wheaties™** ("The Breakfast of Champions")
- **Rice Krispies™** ("the cereal that goes Snap, Crackle and Pop")
- **Quaker Oats™** ("Lowers your Cholesterol")
- . . . and so on.

These slogans, trivial as they seem, are all "Positioning Statements" or "Brand Identities." A positioning statement is a short, punchy, easy-to-remember slogan or tag line about a product that describes a unique property that separates one product from all the others. By the way, there are probably over a thousand breakfast cereals on the market, so competing for your hard-earned dollars is serious business. Only a few brands will dominate your attention and consistently outsell the rest.

How do you choose? Even if you've eaten these products for many years, what is it you remember? Most likely, it boils down to a tag line such as *"Breakfast of Champions"* that always sticks in your mind.

So what does this have to do with job search? In a word, *everything!*

Most job seekers today give scant thought to how they are perceived in the bigger world or how they compare to the hundreds of competitors they face. They address only their own skills—which is like saying that Wheaties™ is made from whole wheat. *So what?*

Most résumés say this about their owner: "I have the skills; I'm a good, smart person and I'll work really hard for you." That describes you and about 2,000 other applicants.

You may be the greatest candidate for the job, but if that's all your résumé has to offer, no one is likely to remember you or invite you for an interview.

And what if an employer *does* call you—*what will you say that will cause you to be memorable even five minutes later?* You're not the only person with great skill sets who's available for hire. Even though you're not selling breakfast cereal, you *are* selling *yourself*, and that means you need to develop a systematic way to package and promote yourself to the bigger world.

Skills aren't enough these days because they're just a feature of what you offer. What you really need to promote are *benefits*.

The "Elevator Pitch"

You've probably heard a version of this example from Sales or Marketing 101:

Imagine walking into an elevator with a hiring manager or high-level executive from an attractive company and she asks you what you do for a living. You have about 20 to 30 seconds to make your pitch. What will you say in that brief time?

Fact is, this is about as much time as your résumé has to make an impression before the reader moves on. It's also about the same amount of time you'll receive at a networking function for your listener to form a first impression of you.

The USP

Your **Unique Selling Proposition (or Presentation)**—your **USP**—describes *the single most unique benefit or value that you offer to an employer*. Consider this a 20-second commercial about yourself. On your résumé, it's a short statement that stimulates the reader's desire to know more about you.

A good USP says, ***"Here's what I can do for you"*** by highlighting *one major benefit* that you bring to this employer.

- This is what you will tell an interviewer during your first phone screen.
- This is what you will tell an interviewer during the beginning of your face-to-face interview.
- This is how you describe yourself in any networking meeting you attend.
- This is what will get you remembered and put you at the top of the pile to "call back."

Once you develop your own USP, boil it down to one short sentence that's both easy to read and easy to speak.

Building **Your** *USP*

As direct marketing expert Perry Marshall says, "If you have a USP or branding statement to offer the world, you're not a commodity any more." In fact, he wasn't talking about some tangible product when he said that—he was talking about *job seekers*. As with marketing products or services to a huge audience, you must think of job search as marketing the product called "You."

The key is to rise above the masses and to know how you can do something that not everybody else can do. What that "something" is, only you can figure out. Nobody can tell you what your USP is. You'll have to "soul search" to identify it for yourself.

Avoid This Common Mistake

Let's use the example of Carol, an administrative assistant. Carol is competing against dozens—if not hundreds—of other administrative assistants, many of them highly skilled. Since the employer has ample candidates to choose from, how does Carol stand out? . . . *with a Unique Selling Proposition*. How can she be different enough to stand out?

Typical tasks for such employees might include answering the phone for the boss, as well as performing various data entry and record-keeping functions. Most people who perform these duties would say something like this: *"I'm an administrative assistant with 20 years' experience,"* Or, *"I'm an administrative assistant who answers phones and knows Excel software."*

Here's the problem: These are just features. They don't tell the interviewer a single thing that makes these candidates unique from everyone else interviewing for this position. Not one benefit has been mentioned that will be realized by the employer from hiring either of them.

Interviewers aren't psychic. You have to sell yourself. Remember, companies only hire employees who are *assets*. With that in mind, let's develop a USP for Carol that sets her apart from everyone else and shows how one "special" trait or skill benefited her company.

Carol is really good at talking with people, answering their questions, and making them feel at ease. Some of the people she talks with are current clients calling in for more information on her company's products. Others may be looking for the support department or even wanting to speak with someone in sales to purchase the product. As a phone person, she's developed a knack for talking with such people and putting them at ease.

Carol's major duty—answering telephones—is just a skill. No big deal. Everybody can answer phones, right? But Carol can go further and transform that simple skill into a *unique benefit* to her prospective employer. Remember, Carol has, in many cases and for many clients, become *"the voice of her company."* Callers readily identify with her and she can demonstrate that many often ask for her by name.

So, how about this to better describe what she *really* does?

"I do relationship-building with clients on the phone."

Now, let's spell out the benefit. We want to show how Carol's particular advantage has specifically benefited the company she has been working for, and we also want to answer the "So what?" question and put an end result to her advantage. Here is the start of what she says:

"I help to cement solid relationships between our clients and my company..."

...and she could actually take this benefit a step further and add: *"and I consistently strengthen the sales link between them and us."*

By framing her USP in this way she leaves no doubt about the nature of how she has benefited her prior company. And guess what? Carol, the administrative assistant, now helps *make money* for her company!

Now here is how Carol's USP might sound:

"I'm a seasoned administrative assistant whose specialty is client-phone relationship-building, creating a solid bond with our clients that strengthens the sales link with my company."

~ ~ ~

Isn't that a whole lot stronger than what we started with?

Here's another quick example. Linda is a Safety and Health Co-ordinator for a government agency. Her role is to:

- *Co-ordinate all safety-related training for 1000+ employees*
- *Ensure compliance with DOT regulations*
- *Co-ordinate and preside over departmental safety meetings*
- *Institute and implement various programs and procedures to improve worker safety and reduce injuries*

That's all very important stuff, but nothing in this list is going to grab the attention of a potential hiring manager. Linda must go further.

Since some of this activity helps save her agency money, she focuses on one of her most important activities. She lowered workers' compensation claims by 37% over a four-year period by her continuous, unwavering enforcement of safety requirements and by training employees at all levels while implementing accountability from the bottom to the top.

By specifying and quantifying, Linda's USP can now become:

"I am a Safety Coordinator with a strength in training and program implementation that helped reduce workers' compensation claims by 37% over a four-year period for my current employer."

Your Personal USP

Now let's get started on *your* USP. You will build your own unique USP by answering the two questions we posed a few pages ago when you completed your Skills Inventory and applied priorities and actions to each skill:

1. **What are (were) the biggest (most important) roles, duties or projects that you performed?**
2. **For each of the items you recorded, how did your employer gain or benefit?**

Here are some examples of how your story might develop.

~ ~ ~

Success story: *Jim developed a test program for a semiconductor chip that identified flaws six months faster than previous tests, resulting in company savings of $200,000.00 in engineers' production time.*

USP becomes: *"I develop test programs for semiconductor chips that identified flaws up to 6 months faster than previous tests and saved my employer over $200,000 to date."*

~ ~ ~

~ ~ ~

Success story: *Betty developed an employee referral program that resulted in three new hires in six months saving the company $90,000.00 in recruiters' fees and Internet job board postings.*

USP becomes: *"I have a strength in developing employee referral programs that resulted in 3 quality hires in 6 months that saved my employer $90,000 in extra hiring costs."*

~ ~ ~

Success story: *As a field applications engineer, Sunil communicated modifications to his company's software product that were requested by his client. This resulted in a new, improved product that brought in $3 million in revenue to his company.*

USP becomes: *"As a strong applications engineer, I was able to quickly identify my client's technical problems and relate them to my design engineers, resulting in an improved product and $3 million revenue for my employer."*

~ ~ ~

Bonus Tip

Always state your USP in terms of money, money, money. Either money you made for the company, money you saved for the company or time you saved that could be translated into money saved by the company. Always try to monetize it (put it into dollar terms). Money gets everybody's attention.

You may have one major strength to develop into a success story and USP, or you may have several that are strong enough to at least consider. Pick the strongest or most impressive one or two and go with them for now. Later you can do the rest, thus adding to your stock of "value added propositions." Use the next two pages to complete the first two statements.

Write a Draft of Your "Success Story" #1:

And Outline Your Unique Selling Proposition #1:

Paycheck 911

Write a Draft of Your "Success Story" #2:

And Outline Your Unique Selling Proposition #2:

Next, polish your work and be ready to use it. It will become what distinguishes you from your competitors—because they probably can't articulate their most basic benefit. And remember, you can do as many of these as you can develop.

Here are some more sample USPs to help stimulate your thinking:

> "I'm a seasoned HR manager with a strength in developing employee referral programs that have netted three quality hires in the last six months, saving my employer $90,000 in recruitment costs."

> "As a seasoned Financial Manager, my strengths combine both Finance/Accounting and Financial Systems used in designing a budgeting and forecasting model, which saved my employer $65.5 million in 10 years."

> "I am an Account Analyst, strong in new account development, from which vantage point I prospected over 8000 accounts, generating $29.3 Million in approved loans for my employer in 15 months."

> "A seasoned Sales Manager, my strength in creative sales and marketing techniques generated $500,000 in brand new revenue for my employer in 12 months."

> "I am a veteran Director of Software Engineering whose strength in planning and execution of large Web-based solutions in healthcare & telecom industries has saved my previous two employers 20% in development costs."

> "As VP of Human Resources, my double strengths in organizational development and people changes enabled me to develop and execute a talent acquisition and management program resulting in sales revenue increases of 60% for one of my clients and $32 million savings for another."

"I have over 13 years of experience as a Mortgage Loan Officer, and my strengths in client relationship building and sales brought in more than $500 million in the past three years and added 3,300 new customer accounts to my current employer's servicing portfolio."

"In the CFO position for more than six years with my current employer, I have become strong in streamlining and automating financial and accounting procedures, saving my firm over $400,000 to date in consulting and personnel costs."

~ ~ ~

Congratulations! You have just completed the first two of what may perhaps become many Unique Selling Propositions that you can use from this moment forward.

You now know how to communicate in proud but accurate terms the most important attribute(s) that you can bring to a company.

Your Résumé

The Four Key Elements Your Résumé MUST Have

Most résumés tell; they don't sell. But they should! As recruiters, we've seen thousands of résumés over the years. Most of them suffer from two critical flaws: 1) they lack focus, and 2) they don't feature clear benefits.

When your résumé is focused, you grab your reader. When you offer clear benefits to your next employer, your résumé sells.

Follow this tried-and-true formula to turn a mediocre résumé into a winning résumé that grabs the attention of the employer and motivates that person to pick up the phone and call you. It's called the *"A-I-D-A"* approach.

What Is A-I-D-A and Why Should I Care?

Your résumé must sell *you*, and that means winning an interview.

As in any sale, before that can happen, several criteria must be met. An easy way to think of this is with the acronym, AIDA, for the natural progression of the psychological changes of the buyer before any sale can take place.

A = Attention

Your résumé must attract the hiring manager's attention. Simply put, a hiring manager must *be able to locate it easily* and must *want to read it*.

I = Interest

Your résumé must quickly get the interest of the reader. You must have elements in your résumé that speak directly to the hiring authority and that answer his or her needs and wants.

D = Desire

You must take your résumé beyond interest by connecting with your reader to motivate them to know more about you.

A = Action!

Finally, your résumé must stimulate action from the reader. This is the close of the sale. The reader will call you for a phone interview or otherwise pass your résumé up the ladder to a decision-maker who has that capability. Before you receive that call, your reader must pass each A-I-D-A step above. Otherwise, it's no sale.

Not only do you need to concern yourself with getting your résumé through the A-I-D-A process, but the clock is ticking as well. Your résumé has about **20 seconds** to grab the reader's Attention, gain their *Interest* and stimulate their *Desire* to know more about you (Action). If your résumé passes the 20-second mark, you have a chance for at least making it to the Action step.

Most résumés are rejected either because the reader didn't feel compelled to continue reading or because the résumé lacked clear benefits or enticing selling points.

To alleviate this, include *all* of the following four critical *marketing elements* that will motivate the reader to call you for an interview.

Marketing Element #1: Focused Objective

A missing or lame **Objective** section can get your résumé tossed in the trash in a matter of seconds. There are too many better résumés out there to bother with yours. Yet most job seekers do a poor job with the Objective.

Toward the top of your résumé, just below your contact information, put your **"Objective."** This is the goal of your job search, the title of the job you are seeking.

Avoid such trite and non-specific objectives as *"Challenging opportunity as a (title) where I can effectively use my managing and sales skills in my ongoing effort to help grow an organization . . . blah, blah . . ."* This is both boring and ineffective. Your résumé has only so much available space and your potential reader so little time. This sort of verbiage does not transmit key information that will widen your net.

The Solution: Use the "Objective" to do one thing, focus on your desired job title. Try this. Under the **Objective** heading, lead off with a clear statement of the title of the position.

Example: **Chief Financial Officer**

Nothing more is needed unless you have job responsibilities that might be defined as several different titles (depending on the company or organization). For instance, you might be a JAVA developer. Within larger companies, it's not uncommon to have concurrent openings for *Java Programmer, Software Developer,* and/or *Software Engineer.* You may qualify for all of these. So, when it's appropriate, list other closely allied titles that the searcher may be seeking. It would be perfectly reasonable in this case to enter the following as the Objective:

Java Programmer, Software Engineer,
Application Developer, Software Developer

By putting several allied (possible) titles in the Objective heading, you may widen your net. Avoid including any unrelated titles or you'll risk appearing unfocused, uncommitted or unskilled.

Marketing Element #2: Keyword Section

Your résumé will be seen by many eyes, including those of electronic scanners. The computer will "score" it by the number of keywords (also known as "buzzwords") the employer will find most relevant. If you don't account for this, your résumé will stay locked in some database while you sit waiting by the phone for the call that never comes.

Everyone pays lip service to this, but few act on it. If you don't, you're missing the boat in two major ways:

- Your résumé needs to be flagged by a computer. To shorten your odds, you need every potential keyword working for you. And not just your skill sets, either. Make sure to add all of your industry buzzwords as well as your biggest soft skills. These are your more general skills that might include "team player," "leadership," "written communication," etc.

- You must appeal to the human that reads your résumé. A reader will scan a great keyword summary section within the first 20 seconds of looking at your résumé. When added to your personal branding statement below, you increase your chances of hooking this reader and getting a more in-depth reading. (Desire to know more).

Solution: Add a *"Keyword Competencies"* Section

A special section called "Keyword Competencies" is not only a great solution for the electronic gatekeeper, but it's also an easily identified and really handy scan section for the human reader.

Focus on the words most likely to be used by either an HR staffing employee or a recruiter. They search résumés by keywords. The higher the number of relevant keywords you can include, the higher relevancy score your résumé will be given. Include a separate section that lists all of the relevant keywords pertaining to your career and skills.

This section should best be listed very near the top of your résumé to introduce and emphasize the skill sets you possess right away. The people who are sorting through potential interview candidates will appreciate this.

What would a "Keyword Section" look like? Here's one defining a *Java Programmer,*

Keyword Competencies: Java • Visual C++ • perl • ticl • application development • visual basic • Windows • NT/XP • programming • GUI • html • project management • layer 2 • BSEE •

> The idea here is to list clearly as many relevant, **searchable** keywords that describe your potential job title and skills. Be sure to include your technical skills, management or organizational skills, relevant software and/or mechanical abilities and expertise. Include anything that might be important to the particular job, including education and tangential but related experience (even if it wasn't accumulated in an "employment" situation but perhaps on a volunteer or community service basis).

> ### Bonus Tips
>
> *Did you know that some of the highest searched keywords today include terms we often overlook? These include many of the "soft skills" like "problem-solving," "leadership," and "verbal and written com-munication." So don't forget to add such skills.*
>
> *~ ~ ~*
>
> *Locate a description of an actual job for which you are applying and copy in all of the applicable buzzwords listed under required and desired skills. This includes education levels. For instance, if they require a BS in Electrical Engineering and you have one, then include "BSEE," as well.*

If you spend some time on this valuable section, you should easily come up with a list of from 40 to 80 relevant searchable keywords to include. By adding relevant keywords, you increase the odds that your résumé will make it onto the "possibles" stack and will get your reader to that "Action" stage—the time when you receive a phone call from a potential employer.

Marketing Element #3—Personal Branding Statement

Let's say you're a CFO or a software project manager or a wedding photographer. Regardless, *what is it that makes you unique, different or better than other applicants?*

Don't think that just having great skill sets or years of experience is going to give you any edge. Lots of other candidates have the same or better skills as you. What to do? Think differently.

Try this example from the real world:

Instead of thinking "car," think "Ultimate Driving Machine."

See what I mean? Call it a slogan, a branding image, a tagline, whatever. When you hear it or see it, you know exactly what the product is and what it might do for you. The best branding images help to sell billions of dollars of product every year. Why? Because they work by promising you a *benefit* for using their product.

What does this have to do with your résumé? Everything.

Too often, candidates think job search is all about selling their specific *skills*. As we emphazied earlier, skills are only commodities; They get you in the door—but they don't win you the job.

HR managers now receive 100 or more résumés per job posting, so it's easy to get lost in the résumé shuffle with lots of other candidates who are competing for that same job—and they all have the same skills as you—and, heaven forbid, some of them may actually be more skilled than you, too. How can you stand out and get selected?

Stop Job Searching and Start Marketing

First of all, does your résumé contain that all-important USP or Branding Statement you developed earlier? Does it contain a clear statement that describes *who you are* and *what benefits an employer gains from hiring you*? Notice what we just said. Does your résumé contain a clear, compelling and attractive statement about *who you are (as opposed to what you have done)*?

If you can develop an honest "slogan" that tells a prospective employer about your "intangible" value as a person, you'll be providing information that fewer than one applicant in a thousand includes, thus giving your prospective employer a glimpse into your worth as a person—which can often be a mighty contribution by an employee to any company. Although we've called this a "branding statement" and a "USP," it may also be described as a *"value added proposition"* that goes well beyond your "core competencies" or your "skill sets."

> *Important Note: Don't confuse either your USP or your Branding Statement with a* **"Summary of Qualifications"**

section that many résumé writers like to include. This section is merely a laundry list of core competencies and does nothing to make you stand out.

As we've pointed out several times so far (but it bears repeating over and over again), the best branding statements usually incorporate *results* in dollars or percentages or amounts of time gained or saved over a certain period.

Here is an alternative example for the CFO whose USP we listed earlier among many examples:

"Seasoned Chief Financial Officer, strong in optimizing organizations to achieve maximum growth and market share, who has saved over $65 million for a single employer over the past eight years."

Does your résumé have this strong a branding statement? Yes, it will take some time to develop a really good statement for yourself, but once you add this to your résumé, you will have moved ahead of most of your competitors.

Now you need one more element for the close: **your business achievements**.

Marketing Element #4: Specific Achievements

Think beyond your skill sets and job duties for as many ways as you can find to deliver "asset value" to your prospective employer.

For instance, suppose you're a video photographer who tapes and edits weddings and special events. You have routinely been taking the additional step of performing all of your post-production work *before* submitting your final results, and this "extra effort" has saved your employer several hundred hours of work. Obviously, this translates into dollars saved, and it's this sort of achievement that you must clearly describe on your résumé.

Our photographer example, highlighting the quantifying "dollar value added" statement, might look like this:

"Saved my employer over $6K in additional labor costs over the past two years by performing post-production work before submitting my final results."

Remember, skills and abilities don't sell. Results do.

Summary

Most résumés are dry documents that read either like a laundry list of job functions or a legal document announcing a local zoning hearing. You can turn your résumé from "dry" to "enticing" by incorporating the four crucial marketing elements we've just discussed.

Remember, you need to move your reader through the complete "A-I-D-A" mental process before they pick up the phone. That means a focused job target and lots of benefits for the employer.

Your Assignment

Before you progress any further, take time to add these four marketing elements to your résumé. It will stand out from the crowd because it no longer just tells. *Now it sells*. More importantly, you'll move a long way toward getting more phone screens and a step closer to the job you really want. If you would like to have the "Job Search Guy" write your résumé, you can go to our website http://www.job444.com/writeres.html and we'll do it for you.

It's time now to revisit those sample résumés on pages 8 through 13 so you can see in practice the four major marketing elements that an effective, selling résumé must have. Each of the two we show varies in ways that reflect the applicant's personality, as well as adapting to the requirements of the individual position. All, however, contain:

- A branding statement
- A keyword summary section
- A clear objective
- Focused achievements and results sections

Go back now and take a look at those well-written, complete résumés that appeared near the front of the book, then return and move forward from here. Mr. Venkat's begins on page 8 and Mr. Cavallo's begins on page 12.

A New Twist— The Video Résumé

A video résumé offers a new tool to get your foot in the door with a growing number of employers today. But could you develop an advantage for yourself by using this medium—could you perhaps stand out from the crowd in this way? Let's investigate.

Also called a *visumé,* a video résumé is a short video of the job seeker essentially selling him or herself to potential employers. Typically, it consists of a short "sales pitch" delivered on-camera that essentially answers the question *"Why should you hire me?"*

Most job seekers film their own videos with a webcam attached to a computer, a camcorder, or a digital camera. They then upload the video to sites on the Web where potential employers might view them.

You'll still need your conventional paper résumé, since video résumés are used primarily to attract attention, helping job seekers stand out among the rising competition on the Web.

Will It Fly?

It remains to be seen whether this new format will take off with actual employers and recruiters, or whether it will fall flat on its face.

Some informal studies have claimed that over 80% of hiring managers or HR managers surveyed replied that they would definitely look at a video résumé if given the opportunity.

And why not? Given a low risk on the part of the employer, it's easy to see how the video format can add a new perspective to an old face—the paper résumé.

Is a Video Résumé for You?

For some time now, early adapting job seekers have been posting their videos directly to Web 2.0 sites such as YouTube® and FaceBook®. Now, video résumés are hitting the mainstream as many of the major job and career sites like CareerBuilder® and Vault® are offering video résumé hosting, and several new companies, including WorkBlast®, are dedicated solely to hosting both employers' and job seekers' videos. In most cases, employers shoulder the costs, and the service is free to candidates.

Are video résumés worth all this fuss? Considering the huge dollar investments supporting this new technology by so many corporations, it may be worth considering on that factor alone. This wouldn't happen unless there were profit and potential time savings for the job search sites and employers.

Although some dissenting voices have been raised within the industry, most notably around possible discrimination concerns, the acceptance has been mostly positive so far.

A Few Pointers

Here is the way it works: As a candidate, you are typically allowed from one to three separate video uploads to these sites, in addition to uploading your conventional résumé.

You can link your video to your full bio, including your "real" résumé. Employers can perform the usual keyword searches and view the resulting videos before looking at the résumés. For the candidates they wish to learn more about, it's an easy click to their full bio.

If you are thinking about creating a visumé of your own, your main advantage will be increased exposure. Employers will be more likely to view a short 1- to 2-minute clip than to paw through hundreds of paper résumés. Also, this method opens up a new *visual element* that can play to your advantage, and it is well known that the more of a person's senses you can engage, the more interest they will have in you and what you are saying.

The downside is that you can appear unprepared—or even downright foolish. For example, in the fall of 2006, a Yale graduate sent his video to a major Wall Street investment firm and later found his video posted on YouTube®, mocked throughout the Internet for its preposterous, bragging style.

Although all that's required to record your own video is a digital video recording device that can upload to the Web, it helps to know what you're doing. Contrary to its name, a video résumé is not your résumé on video. It's actually a short promo enticing the employer to take a look at your "real" résumé online. Before you begin, think of your video project as a short trailer for a new movie. The best movie trailers contain all the action elements necessary to entice you to see the movie itself. Same with your video. It should be brief and to the point.

There is a certain amount of free advice available in books and on the Internet, but you may wish to invest in some direct education to guide you through the scripting and recording process. In fact, some individuals in higher-level executive positions are hiring producers who charge up to $3,500 for a professionally produced video.

Most candidates won't need such a production, but some forethought in planning and scripting would be well advised. This is a new technology still in the infant stage. No doubt, it will evolve considerably in the coming years.

Nine Mistakes You Shouldn't Make In Your Video

A video résumé could get your foot in the door of that "just right" company. Don't end up with egg on your face, though. Before you make that video, check out these 9 common mistakes and how you can avoid each one.

1. **It runs too long** — Don't bore the hiring managers. Your video should be a short, inspiring pitch. Think "Less is More." Keep it under two minutes, preferably about one minute, which should usually be sufficient to get your message across.

2. **You don't know who you are** — Prepare your "elevator pitch" before you record. Commonly known as a USP, or Unique Selling Proposition, this is a one-sentence pitch that describes the single biggest benefit that you bring to a potential employer. For example: *"I'm a seasoned Sales Manager whose strength in creative sales and marketing technique generated $500,000 in brand new revenue for my employer in 12 months."*

3. **Thinking a video résumé is your résumé on video** — Contrary to its name, a video résumé is *not* a résumé. It's a 30 to 60-second ad spot to entice your viewers to look at your (digital) résumé to find out more about you.

4. **Rambling on camera** — Put it on paper first. Think of what you want to say about yourself. Write it down in short sentences, then say it out loud. Replace any syntax problems or phrases that are hard to say. You speak differently than you write, so keep it in a conversational tone, as if you were speaking to your real-life interviewer a few feet away.

5. **Too many "ums and ahs"** — Don't wing it. Your finished product should be compelling. This is the most professional image you want to present, so prepare ahead of time and memorize your script. This won't be hard since it should only be about a half to three quarters of a page in length and only cover a few simple points. Remember, you won't have notes in the interview room, either.

6. **Severe case of "Serious Face"** — Have a bit of fun with it. You want to project enthusiasm. Think "Upbeat" and smile when you look into the camera. Imagine that you are meeting with a flesh and blood hiring manager at a great company who already likes what she sees.

7. **Giving far too much information** — Remember the "KISS" Formula (Keep It Simple, Stupid). You want to whet their appetites to know more. Give them just enough info to

tantalize them. End with an invitation to check out even more interesting info on your résumé.

8. **Uninviting appearance** — Remember that a video résumé is a type of interview, *so dress the part*. Give the appearance of someone in the role you're applying for. You will also have some background showing on the video. Make sure it's not your dirty laundry or the clutter of your bedroom. Try standing against a relatively bare wall. You want them looking at you, not at what's behind you.

9. **Too many "Clowns"** — No folded arms or hands on hips—and be careful about all gesturing. While it's OK to use your hands to accentuate, watch out for those "clowns," which is what acting coaches call unnecessary repetitive arm movements that, on playback, tend to make you appear like a clown, i.e., humorous. You don't want unintentional laughs. Keep your arms and hands by your side as much as possible.

Summary

Video résumés are offering a new wrinkle to the job search process because they offer both time savings to hiring managers and HR people—and they add a new dimension to candidate evaluation for employers and recruiters alike.

At this point, the added exposure you may receive could be reason enough to add a video résumé to your job search approach. The major caveat is to educate yourself to produce as high a quality product as you can. Remember, if you post your video to an online video site, it may be viewed by thousands of people across the world, so "put your best face forward."

Your video résumé can open new doors for you, or it can inadvertently slam them in your face. By observing these few rules, you have the opportunity to let potential employers see the real "you," as you intended.

Section III -- RESEARCH

In this section you will learn about resources available to you as you develop the "marketplace" for your job hunt—the media and the companies most likely to bring you to the "paydirt" stage of your efforts.

Research

You may have approached your job search—like many thousands before you—by throwing a résumé together and immediately searching at the usual watering holes, which included the job posting sites and the career and employment sections of various corporate websites. After weeks or perhaps months, the realization settles in that you're not achieving your goal, which was a great job. Like many before you, you may have even reached that horrible, depressing state called "settling." You'll settle for most *any* job.

Finding Jobs, "Hidden" or Posted

You needn't settle any more, as long as you're willing to do some extra work for your dreams. You can get your dream job, or even just a better job, if you put forth the effort. Take some of the specific action steps we are about to recommend. Each one will put you in touch with the so-called "Hidden Job Market." Actually, it's not so much a "hidden" job market; rather, it's *not approached*.

You've probably read or heard that 80% of jobs today are filled outside of the Internet. This may conjure up images of some huge underworld black market operation where jobs are mysteriously traded in dark alleyways.

The truth is, it's all rather upfront and taking place every day through something called networking, which takes many forms and includes formal networking meetings and organizations but can also mean getting together for coffee or lunch with a new contact.

It also means *linking through the Internet* using such sites as LinkedIn®, Facebook®, or StumbledUpon®. It could even be connections through a hobby, a shared interest, or a sports connection (golf is the cliché here) that blossoms into an interview.

We'll talk about more formal ways to network with the intention of making focused inquiries about the marketplace. We'll also look at ways to put your name and accomplishments in front of people who have inside information and power and who can help you move into this hidden job market.

1. Online Job Development Resources
Traditional Online Resources

You've most likely posted your résumé to several of the online posting sites. The favored approach of job seekers, sending résumés to online sources is a good start, but not enough to get into the "loop" and uncover the unposted jobs. This is the "Point and Click" method of job searching and it won't get you the all-important conversations you want with insiders and decision-makers. Also, it won't get you insider referrals. It *will* heighten your competition, include you with the masses and reduce you to playing the "buyers' market" of job search.

Using the traditional Internet sources to find jobs online is an important adjunct that you want to cover, but you don't want to invest the majority of your time here. Be aware that there are probably hundreds of sites where you can find jobs online on the Internet. At this writing, we've included these top job/résumé posting and career/job search information & advice sites with a few up-and-comers included.

Check out these sites and post your résumé with those you feel are the most appropriate. Some, like Monster[R] and CareerBuilder[R], offer a "Search Agent" which is a method to notify you by e-mail when a new job is posted that matches your search criteria.

Monster[R] — Starting to feel competition from several sites below but still the granddaddy and largest of all the online job sites. Also offers job search and career advice.

Careerbuilder[R] — Owned by the Gannett Co. Offers both print and online job search and advice services partnering with 150 newspapers as well as AOL and MSN.

Paycheck 911

Hotjobs® — A division of Internet giant Yahoo®. Has a huge job search site plus offers an extensive tools and advice section for career and job search improvement.

WorkGiant® — An up-and-comer, this pay-for-performance site allows employers to post all jobs for free, *plus pays job seekers referral fees of from $50 to $200 each for all candidates who are hired.*

Indeed® — Another up-and-comer, this is billed as a one-stop search engine for jobs. Simply list your job preferences and get a slug of returns pulled from many other sites, including those listed here. No résumé posting (visibility) here, though.

CareerOneStop (formerly America's Job Bank) — A U.S. Department of Labor-sponsored website that offers career resources and workforce information to job seekers.

CraigsList® — founded by Craig Newmark in 1995, began posting high tech jobs online that he and a few others became aware of in the Silicon Valley area. What started as a small underground jobs and information networking bulletin board has since flourished into a large jobs/personals data site that offers a more personal touch and is now highly targeted to many major cities throughout the country. If you live in or near a major city (including outside the U.S.), you should find a local site devoted to your area.

Workblast® — is another up-and-comer. As with other job sites, they link candidates with thousands of employers. They've added an interesting twist. Job seekers can easily make and upload up to 3 video résumés along with their conventional digital résumé and store them on the company server for later viewing by potential employers. An added bonus: candidates can watch an employer video to discover more about the company before applying. The service is free to candidates.

JobMaps® — combines Indeed.com resources with Google® Maps; this is a job search engine that allows you to see where jobs are located on a map.

SimplyHired® — Billing themselves as the "one-stop searching" website, they boast the world's largest job search engine. Can also cross-search LinkedIn® for any contacts within your network from any company you search. They aggregate data from multiple sources including large and small job boards as well as newspaper classified listings.

JobFox® — Founded by ex-CareerBuilder® execs, this site offers a unique way of posting and formatting your résumé. This site rebuilds your résumé to an attractive one-page format that pulls out relevant info and gives it a spiffy webpage look. Another feature is that it gives you an up-to-the-minute knowledge about which employers have looked at your résumé.

Web 2.0 and Social Networking Resources

The Internet continues to evolve as an entity, partly through advancing technology but also in the way people relate to it and use it in their lives. No doubt, you've already posted your résumé on major job sites such as Monster®, HotJobs® and CareerBuilder®. Now it's time to go further, thanks to something called "**Web 2.0**."

Although this isn't the place to become involved in a major discussion of software and Web development technology, it might be useful to at least acknowledge the *Web 2.0* evolution. This has become the term to describe the so-called "second generation Web."

Basically, Web 2.0 websites allow users to do more than just retrieve information. They can add to the interactive facilities of "Web 1.0" to provide what has been termed the "Network as Platform" style computing. This allows users to now run software applications entirely through their browsers. Think of Web 1.0 as the old one-sided "Web as information source," whereas, Web 2.0 now allows you as a user *to participate.*

Most Web 2.0 sites are run on something called AJAX. This is a specific group of Web development technologies that make it possible to create interactive Web applications by exchanging relatively small amounts of data with the server on a "while you wait" basis— without having to reload the page or redirect you to a new page. This makes for a faster, more user-satisfying experience.

So what does Web 2.0 mean to you, the job hunter?

It means that you now have a wider degree of access to the Web for the purposes of posting your résumé or "profile" than you did even a few short years ago. In fact, the landscape continues to change even as we write. Here is a listing of some of the major Web 2.0 sites you need to be aware of and to incorporate into your job hunt marketing efforts:

LinkedIn®

A business-oriented networking site, LinkedIn® is one of the many Web networking sites designed to connect business people with one another. If you were to be on just one social networking site, LinkedIn® would be your number one choice. As of this writing, LinkedIn® is the largest and most often used or mentioned social network, with over 16 million registered users. The purpose of LinkedIn® is to allow a user to maintain a personal list of contact details of other business people they know. Called "Connections," a user can invite others they know to become connections, as well.

"Connections" can be used to build up a contact network that can grow exponentially through the connections of your contacts. The goal is to facilitate an introduction to someone you would like to meet through one of your trusted contacts. You can also use your connections to find jobs, contacts and business opportunities.

Use LinkedIn® to look for jobs

You can now use LinkedIn® to search for jobs that have been posted by hiring managers who are current LinkedIn® users.

You have a wide array of criteria to use when setting up your search, even limiting by zipcode to find jobs located near you. You can use the search results in one of two ways.

1. First, you can apply to the job directly by submitting a personalized cover letter, adding your contact information and uploading your résumé. Much the same as you would when you submit to any job posted on the Internet.

2. The other way to apply is to ask for an introduction to the hiring manager listed by one of your connections. The upside of going this route is that you rise from the masses through the benefit of a mutual contact. The downside is that unless you have a number of well-connected contacts, the odds are that your invitation may not be accepted.

Register and enter your profile on LinkedIn®

If you haven't done so already, register on LinkedIn® and spend some time building your profile. Upload a good, businesslike photo of yourself. Complete each section on your personal stats, education and professional employment from current to past positions. Here are a few pointers:

- Consider LinkedIn® as a group of people coming together at the end of a busy day to connect and see what's happening in other people's worlds.
- People aren't looking for a heavy-duty sales pitch.
- Think of it as a friendly cocktail party rather than some Chamber of Commerce networking event where everyone is flashing their business cards.

With these thoughts in mind, write a brief, friendly approach on your profile, especially in your summary section. Pretend you're at a party and you're introducing yourself for the first time. You're not going to be flashing your résumé. Rather, you'll have a few short sentences to describe yourself. Here is where your USP can come into play. People only want a short, catchy sentence or two that describes you.

LinkedIn® also gives you a number of parameters offering an introduction or a connection when you fill out your intial online profile. Among other possibilities, your desire for connections may include a job opportunity, a business venture or just making new connections. Check all that apply.

Paycheck 911

Be aware that if you are currently employed, it's possible that your boss or supervisor may view your profile, and it will clearly show that you are looking for a new job opportunity if you checked that particular box.

Listing your educational background, job titles, past employers' names and specific industry-related keywords in your LinkedIn® profile will work to your advantage. As with résumé postings to actual job sites, your profile may be pulled via keyword search by recruiting firms and hiring managers who regularly use LinkedIn® as a candidate source for their open positions.

Your LinkedIn® profile offers you a link to which you can refer people whenever a conversation you're having—anywhere—steers toward possible employment opportunities.

You can customize your profile with as much or as little information as you wish. You can even select a personalized URL and note it on a business card that you can pass to selected individuals you meet. You can also use your personalized LinkedIn® URL in your e-mail signature. This is a much better form of contact than the old "I need a job!" method of pulling out or e-mailing your résumé to someone you've only just met or contacted.

For those who do blog, there is a Wordpress® plugin called "LinkedIn_hResume" to display your LinkedIn® profile in your Wordpress® blog in your own customized design.

Myspace®

Founded in 2003, Myspace® has grown to over 200 million users at this writing. According to Wikipedia®, Myspace® has an Alexa® ranking of the 6th most visited site in the world, sometimes topping out at number one, depending on the week in question.

Designed as one of the first social networking sites designed to bring people together, Myspace® has attracted a huge youth demographic in its user base. Used primarily to collect and attract "friends," users can customize their personal page to their own "look-and-feel" needs. Since Myspace® is heavily youth culture-based, the profiles are defaulted to standard *"About Me"* and *"Who I'd Like to Meet"* sections.

You can enter your education under schools as well as any companies you have worked for, once again under a separate *"Company"* section. And since over 200 million people currently use Myspace®, recruiting firms and employers are beginning to fish the Myspace® pond. It makes sense to register and set up your profile.

You'll need to carefully navigate the social waters in the "my favorite" this and that sections in deciding which, if any, of the categories listed makes sense for you to incorporate on your profile. My guess is that over time, Myspace® will probably adopt more business-friendly features such as full résumé profiling ability, given the organization is now owned by News Corporation, which is the parent of the Fox companies and the home of Rupert Murdoch.

Facebook®

Playing second fiddle to Myspace®, Facebook® doesn't do badly, pulling an Alexa® ranking of 7, right behind competitor Myspace®— also according to Wikipedia®.

Formed in 2004, Facebook® was originally restricted to users with a university (.edu, etc.) e-mail address. Only since 2006 has Facebook® allowed access to anyone over the age of 13.

Like Myspace®, Facebook® is heavily geared to the twenty-somethings and oriented toward the social aspects of university life. There are currently almost 60 million users. Also like Myspace®, you can build a personal profile including your education, and current and past employers.

Like LinkedIn®, you can edit the layout of your profile and upload your photo. Take the time now to add your profile and work history to Facebook®, avoiding all the more childlike sections on "my favorite TV shows," etc.

Recruiters and employers are regularly trolling these social networking sites, even creating corporate pages of their own, although the main focus of Facebook® is that it's a place to "hang out." I doubt there is much interest in some stuffy corporate presence trying to be hip in the neighborhood. Still, it seems to have become more mainstream (business) oriented in the past year or so.

Since money talks and corporations will invest in connecting with the watering holes where their future employees hang out, more changes will certainly occur, making this a more meaningful networking avenue for direct job search as time progresses.

Check out the *"Applications"* link for literally scores of special applications to run with Facebook®. Most notably, *"My Résumé"* is a Facebook® application that lets you post your Linkedin® profile or your résumé on Facebook®.

Kickstart®

Kickstart® (www.kickstart.yahoo.com) is owned by Yahoo!®. Being the most heavily visited website on the planet, Yahoo® has intentions of growing Kickstart® into a serious networking site akin to LinkedIn®. Kickstart®'s edge or "angle" is the slant toward college connections. This could be beneficial, especially when connecting to alumni from your alma mater. This could also be a drawback for those without university degrees, who would have no reason to participate. If you have the degree, sign up and post your profile.

While Kickstart® doesn't have the information capabilities that LinkedIn® has, it will no doubt grow as a social networking force in the coming years if, for no other reason than that it's backed by the huge resources of Yahoo!®

Blogs

A blog is one of the most relevant tools used to promote awareness. Essentially a platform to espouse thoughts, ideas, opinions, attitudes and information, a blog can be a great device to attract attention to you and to help establish yourself as a thought leader in your industry or profession. If you're in a position that's cutting edge, technology-based, or has high visibility, or if you're a journalist—or a natural born writer—then a blog may be an ideal way to generate interest and traffic.

Often, I see the recommendation made to job hunters to develop a blog of their own because of its obvious benefits in these areas. Unfortunately, creating a blog will be technically beyond the abilities of most people. Even with that hurdle surmounted, there is still the question, *"What if you build it and nobody comes?"*

Once established, your blog will need to generate considerable traffic to and from the sort of audience you seek to engage. You might be able to accomplish this by cross-linking to your LinkedIn® profile, cross-posting to other relevant blogs and posting your opinions on professional forums on the Web and leaving your blog link in all cases. Most of the blog-building sites (blogger.com, blogspot.com and others) have easy-to-follow instructions on how to do these sorts of things.

The upside of blogs is the increase in credibility and exposure you gain on the Web. The downside includes the technology hurdle, the expense (usually quite modest, sometimes free, but you'll need to search the Internet for the blog-builder you like), and the time required to write valuable content once a week or more in your area of expertise.

One way of using blogs to your advantage without having to develop your own blog is to find notable (A-level) bloggers in your professional space and read their posts on a regular basis to get a feel for them and their audience. You can easily do this by loading the free Google® and Alexa® toolbars onto your computer. Using these free services, you can assemble valuable traffic information on your blog.

A Google® page rank of 5 or higher, for instance, indicates that a site has a high degree of relevance. The higher the number (up to 10), the higher the relevance, or importance, that the site commands within its particular niche. An Alexa® ranking of five figures (XX,XXX) or less indicates that a fair number of people are reading the blog.

If the numbers warrant it, you might want to occasionally post a comment of your own to the site. It should be content-oriented and apply strictly to the topic of the article. Sign with your name and a link to your LinkedIn® profile (see below). This will give you exposure as a knowledgeable source in your field. More importantly, it gives you a link back to your profile, which (of course) includes your summary and résumé. The added benefit is that you're getting eyeball exposure from the movers and shakers in your industry or field.

2.   *Researching the Hidden Job Market*

Would You Rather Be in a "Buyer's" or a "Seller's" Market?

Let's start with some basics:

The Buyer's Market Approach to a job search is the worst way to conduct a job search. It consists of relying on the following activities:

- Flooding your résumé over the Internet individually or through résumé 'blasting' services
- Randomly mailing résumés without first contacting the recipient (Think SPAM)
- Answering want ads of any kind (Square pegs in round holes)
- Randomly contacting search firms and hoping you'll match their clients' job openings (what do you know about the recruiters there? Do you really understand how they work and whether they actually have first-rate contacts in your industry?)

The Seller's Market Approach to job search is the better way to job hunt. It consists of relying on any and all of the following activities:

- Generating referrals from family, friends, etc.
- Networking in-person as well as using social software such as LinkedIn®, Kickstart® and others
- Research using specific research tools, databases and compiled lists to ID companies and organizations that most interest you

- Locating names, titles and contact information of people within these companies that you can contact with letters of inquiry and follow-up phone contacts
- Developing conversations with these people to generate leads, industry information, referrals and interviews
- Purchasing (renting) a custom compiled list of companies, and the names and titles of contacts to which you can market, as mentioned above
- Joining professional or trade organizations and networking within

Informational interviewing

In a following chapter, we'll talk about putting it all together by merging the product called "you" with people who have titles and who function as decision-makers in the outside world. These people can help you by giving you leads, referrals and—most importantly—interviews for your next great job.

Building your list and finding names you can market to

The job search market has certainly become more competitive.

No doubt you've already spent several weeks or more doing job search using the "point & click" method. In other words, you've developed a résumé and posted it to every job site or corporate website that has advertised an opening for which you felt qualified.

OK, so the phone hasn't exactly been ringing off the hook, has it?

Here's part of the problem: everybody else has seen and responded to those same job ads. Many employers report receiving over 100 résumés for each job opening. You're just one of a huge number. When you *do* receive a call, be assured that the employer is calling 20 or more other candidates for that same opening, and you'll be competing with numbers of other people who want this job as much or more than you. This is called a "buyers' market." You don't want to function here because you're a commodity with little leverage.

Paycheck 911

When you realize that the vast majority of job openings are not advertised, we suggest that you steer away from the "buyer's market" entirely by doing some research up front.

The purpose of this research is to determine the types of companies you actually want to work for. Then you'll research each of these companies—and their competitors. But before you get there, start with a free tool to help you widen your company search. It's called the Alexa® Tool Bar. You can download it for free, and it will give you all sorts of info from almost any corporate website you look up. It will also give you a listing of like companies (often their competitors).

You'll learn about a number of other more powerful tools and resources to help you identify the right companies that might need your skills and accomplishments.

For example, a good basic resource is Lead411®. It will cost about $30/month, but is well worth the price. You'll also learn more about specific business references and databases offered in your local library for free. These include references such as Hoovers®, ThomasNet®, EBSCO® and Standard & Poor's®. Typically, these references are accessed by private individuals and business people on a subscription-basis and cost as much as $5,000 for a yearly subscription.

Your local library will probably have most of these in the reference section. If so, you can use them for free. Typically, you'll look for familiar companies to start with. Find out what their SIC (or NAIC) code is. This is important for sources such as S&P, which are cross-indexed by this code. Then look up all companies in those particular SICs. Make a list of the companies and their locations.

Once you've compiled an extensive list of companies, you'll learn how to use the social networking site LinkedIn® as well as the business research sites Spoke® and ZoomInfo®. Although free at the basic level, I would advise you to invest in their enhanced or premium services for a month or so to find the names and full contact information of potential hiring managers and decision-makers in these companies.

Try to find mid-level managers in the larger corporations. For smaller companies, aim for the VP in your most relevant line of work.

You can also purchase a custom list of names from a list provider. Once you know the SIC codes for the companies you'd like to work for, buy a list from a list supplier such as Zapdata® (or equivalent list vendor that you can find on the Internet). These providers will allow you to limit your search by zipcode to find all of the companies in a particular geographic area.

You'll end up with at least one or more names, titles and complete contact information for every potential hiring manager or decision-maker within each company you've targeted. This custom list may cost you from $30 to $100 or more, but it may be well worth the investment if it proves to be the difference between taking *any* job and landing *the right job*—the one you really want.

You'll then target these people with a short, personalized Letter of Inquiry. Two or three short paragraphs is adequate. Tell your prospective employer in one sentence what makes you different or special. Include a $$ figure, if possible. Companies always rate more highly those employees who have either made or saved them money. Identify how you've done that, then develop some examples from your past.

Don't include a résumé at this point. Follow up with them in three days or so.

Is this easy work? Not necessarily. But the tangible benefits of approaching your job search this way are great.

First, you've taken yourself out of the herd. And second, you've established yourself as an individual by demonstrating that you have something special to offer. You're unique, not just a number or a piece of paper.

Will you face some rejection? Yes, but you've already faced indifference and rejection by continuing to use the "buyer's market" approach to job search that virtually every other job seeker uses when they apply to Monster®/corporate/recruiter postings. More importantly, you'll also hit pay dirt with either an interview or a referral to a "hot lead."

I'm not just promoting some ivory tower stuff here. I've used this very technique myself several times in my own career when my back was against the wall, job postings weren't cutting it, and I desperately needed to find a way to get in front of decision-makers that WORKED. This method works, not only for me but for many, many others as well.

Am I saying to totally stop applying to Monster® and corporate Web postings? Absolutely not. However, when you incorporate this approach you will be much closer to winning either an interview or referrals to a good opportunity.

The advantage of this technique is that you are now a seller in a seller's market. You'll greatly limit—if not totally eliminate—any competition you would ordinarily face from the hordes of candidates who would have already sent their résumé.

Do You Really Want to Work There?

Most job search approaches are "Ready! Fire! Aim!" Don't do it.

Do Your Research First

What happens in the real job search world is that most job seekers, in the interest of generating a lot of search "activity," will throw a bunch of résumés up against the wall to see what sticks. Knowing that job search is a numbers game, they think that a certain percentage will fall their way, so why not stack the deck up front and follow up with those that "stick?"

Here Are Two Big Problems with That Thinking:

1. If you haven't done the basic research beforehand, you'll be caught dead in the water if you don't have any basic knowledge about the company or the job opportunity, should a call come through for an initial phone screen. You'll look foolish, and worse, you're now toast. You've just been ruled out of contention after a five-minute phone call. Your résumé will immediately be tossed onto the "reject" pile as the interviewer moves on to call the next candidate.

2. Your résumé is an application to work at this company. If you haven't put any forethought into learning about the company you've applied to, you won't be able to make good judgments about the suitability of the company to your needs and wants. And even if you're offered a first interview, waiting until after you have interviewed could put you in a more emotionally vulnerable state. Feeling more desperate to make some change now, you may tend to overlook certain negatives that creep up once you become caught up in the excitement of the interview process and the possibilities of change.

Take this example from my own career: Many years ago I was working for a large pharmaceutical company and desired a change to a more dynamic company. After a few months of being "available," I had an opportunity to work for a company I knew little about. I interviewed, let myself get caught up in the excitement, and ignored the nagging doubts that told me the job responsibilities were not right. I accepted the job offer and spent most of the next 11 months hating my new job. It was a great company, but it was just a bad fit with my personality. I knew this AFTER I started interviewing, but I found it hard to say "no." If I had done my research ahead of time, I never would have considered this opportunity.

Take a lesson from me: research *before* you leap, when you're calm and rational and can focus your time and energy on those specific companies and opportunities that are a good fit.

You should answer these basic questions:

- How large is the company?
- What products/services do they offer?
- Who are their competitors?
- Where do they rank in their market?
- What is their financial situation?

The advantage of knowing this information up front is that it will put you in a power position when you DO receive a call from an employer. You're now able to talk intelligently about the company, the opportunity and products, and to use this information to generate a knowledgeable *conversation* with your caller. This signifies *interest* and gets you to the next stage: a more in-depth phone screen or a face-to-face interview.

Resources to Find Basic Information:

- Corporate websites (see also their Press Release section).
- The Reference Section of your local public library where you can check out resources such as: Hoover's®, Thomasnet®, EBSCO®, and Standard & Poor's®, among others.

- *The Business Journal*™, local trade or business papers (also see your library).

Talk with People (*social software, network*).

Be current on a company before you even send your résumé. Find out earlier rather than later whether you would actually like to work for a particular company. It can make all the difference if you do the legwork up front rather than leaving it to chance late in the interview stage. Use the Web 2.0 resources we discussed earlier.

Take Ownership of Your Job Search

Take an active role in your job search. You can't just sit by the phone. You need to work hard to find the right job for yourself. You might even want to remind yourself that searching for a job is the hardest job you'll ever have. The reason is simple—when it's done *right,* it's full of rejection.

Wrong Approach:

Too many job seekers, in the interest of AVOIDING REJECTION, will simply search all the job sites, post a résumé to a few opportunities listed, and then sit back and wait. This is the passive, no-win approach to job search that will never get you the results you are looking for. Don't let yourself fall into this role.

Better Approach:

Quite the contrary, you need to *invite rejection.* Each "No" you receive will bring you closer to a "Yes." It's in your best interest to get past each "No" as quickly as possible. Don't dawdle, and don't avoid the not-so-fun task of hearing that awful word "No."

Remember, you're looking for the Job that YOU Really Want. That means you're going to have to dig to find it. It's not on a silver platter, it's possibly not on some job site—or even on the Web. You are going to have to expend some energy during a several week (or month) period of time.

You'll take ownership of your job search in two ways:

1. Locate new information

Taking ownership means taking a proactive approach to your job search. We've already talked about researching companies you want to work for without regard to whether a specific job may have been posted. You also know about using business resources such as Lead411®, EBSCO®, Standard & Poor's®, Hoover's®, ThomasNet® and many others.

2. Once you have developed a target list of possible companies, you should locate appropriate people within those companies you can contact initially.

Three great Internet networking tools to accomplish this are LinkedIn®, Spoke® and ZoomInfo®. Focus on employees with whom you might easily make an initial contact within your area of expertise.

For example, if you are a software developer, you might want to focus on individuals with management function in the areas of software development, project management, director of operations, or even the VP of engineering (if the company is small). Once you've combined the corporate and employee information and compiled your list, you can make the all-important next step.

Contacting and Following Up with People

At this point, you're going to have to stick your neck out a bit. That means picking up the phone and actually calling the people that you have identified. Once you've sent a Letter of Inquiry or a résumé to an individual, don't expect your phone to ring. Wait a couple of days, then pick up the phone and call them to see if they can speak with you for a few minutes.

Summary

The advantage of a proactive job search approach is that most other job seekers, *your competitors,* will *not* be doing this. Other job seekers are passive. They write a résumé, look up today's available jobs on the Internet, post their résumé qualifications, then sit back and wait. When the phone doesn't ring, they move on and start all over again, posting their résumé to the same jobs as all the other job seekers. Not much of a future, if you're looking for a job that's right for *you*. The lesson is to never leave your success in the hands of strangers. Take charge of your job search right now and blaze new trails that others don't tread.

Research Tools

You'll Need Alexa®

You can avoid hours of frustrating and wasted research by using a Recruiter's Secret that, with one simple, *FREE* tool will easily widen your prospective employer list and locate dozens of *TARGETED* new companies you can contact. In less than 30 minutes, you'll widen your job search five times over, pinpointing the companies that are right for you, while cutting down on hours of wasted research!

Here's the scoop: Alexa® is an Internet services company, now owned by Amazon.com®, that provides dynamic data about the Web. They list their services to include "website traffic information, statistics, and other tools to make timely and intelligent business and consumer decisions."

There is one very useful item that they offer at no cost: *the Alexa® Toolbar*. So start with a visit to their site at http://www.alexa.com. On the menu at the left side margin, you'll notice a "download" button for the "Alexa® Toolbar." Press this button and follow the simple instructions to download and install the toolbar to your browser. (Note: at this writing, Alexa®, unfortunately, hasn't developed a version of the toolbar for Mac users, and they were currently working on a version for Microsoft Windows Vista®.)

This toolbar will give you a broad range of statistics on the websites you visit. Generally, it will rank each site according to its popularity by total number of visits. More importantly for the job seeker, the Alexa® Toolbar will open new worlds by uncovering a wide array of new companies to explore and helping you to determine which ones you will follow up with.

This idea is so important that we'd like you to *download the toolbar—right now*. Then return here and we'll walk you through it.

~ ~ ~

Ready?

Once it is installed, you'll notice that across the top of the Alexa® Toolbar there are several buttons. We're going to use some of these features to make our research easier.

Let's start by looking up a simple, straightforward example, a company everyone knows—www.google.com.

The first button is labeled "info." Push this and a new window will appear containing more detailed information on Google® (or whatever site you are on at the moment). Pushing the button attached to it (showing two black "down" arrow keys) will give you detailed contact info on this particular company. In this case, we access address, phone numbers and specific ranking info.

To the left of the "info" button there is a number (2, in this case). This means Google® is the second-highest-ranking site on the Internet, at least according to Alexa®'s ranking, which is probably correct. To the right of this rank indicator, you'll see a button with arrows on it and also a button with two black "down" arrows. Pressing this button gives you a window with more details on this particular site.

When you scroll down, you also will see a list that has the heading: *"People who visit this page also visit:"* Under this you will see a list of 10 similar companies. Each one is conveniently linked so that you can right-click and select "open in new window" to check them out.

Furthermore, by clicking on the connecting button with two black "down" arrows, you will see a list of 11 companies, all linked, that you can immediately look up.

If that weren't enough, below the lists there are two headings:

Categories and ***Industries***

Both are highly searchable and can provide you with a wide-ranging list of companies that are similar to—or competitive with—Google®.

Now try this specifically with some of the companies you have been applying to.

Hands-On Example:

Let's say you're interested in an opening with "Quantum Corporation." On the Alexa® Toolbar, Look up www.quantum.com, then look across to find the list of companies that people also visit when they search for "Quantum Corporation." By pressing on the "down" arrow button to the left of the two companies listed, a window listing about ten company links will appear. Pressing the "*More Related Links*" button at the bottom of that window will bring you to another view of 20 company links that you can click on to do further research.

You'll find that most of these companies are in the same industry, offering the same or similar types of products and services. Take note of who these companies are and start making a list for your next level of research.

Now take that list of companies and look up each one of them in turn, and do the same. You'll see how quickly you can come up with a long list of potential new companies to prospect.

You can also cull this information from corporate resources such as Hoover's® and others (free at your library) or even ZoomInfo® or Spoke® at the paid level.

Your goal is to generate a large list of potential companies or organizations that might best need your skills and accomplishments.

You'll also need a corresponding list of potential hiring managers or decision-makers within those companies that you can contact directly.

Let's continue our research and build on your initial list developed from Alexa®. While Alexa® is a good start, it is not very useful in pinpointing the number of companies that you'll be needing for your marketing.

Lead411®

For a monthly fee of under $30, you can sign up for Lead 411®, (**www.lead411.com**), and you can unsubscribe at any time after your first month. You'll receive the basic service, which is a virtually unlimited search capability to all the companies across the U.S. You will have access to:

1) The address, phone numbers, names and titles of upper management (often including their e-mail addresses—*but don't e-mail them*).

2) A brief synopsis of their mission and services/products.

3) Company vitals, including the number of employees, annual revenues, and number of available jobs listed currently on their website.

It can also link you directly to the corporate website. You can print these pages and file for later use. They let you check it out for free for one day, then *you* make the call.

After your initial research with Alexa®, follow up with more in-depth research using Lead411®. You will begin amassing pages of information to track down.

As you find out more about a particular company, add this new information to your company folder. You will use it later in your contact and interviewing stage.

Once you've compiled a significant list of target companies, you'll need to use some different resources to find names and titles of people. This is where Spoke®, ZoomInfo® and LinkedIn® can prove valuable for their ability to generate names, titles and actual contact information on mid to lower-level employees. This includes potential hiring managers.

LinkedIn®

We've already mentioned a bit about LinkedIn® and how you can use it to list yourself and your résumé. But there's more. You can access LinkedIn® for names of people you can contact in your outward marketing efforts to find those "hidden jobs." Described as a "well-heeled social club," LinkedIn® targets business users, and it does so at many levels, from upper-echelon managers and executives down to the mid-level managers and even "worker bees," all of whom are now listing themselves in LinkedIn®. As of this writing, LinkedIn® is the largest and most often used or mentioned social network, with over 16 million registered users.

The purpose of LinkedIn® is to allow a user to maintain a personal list of contact details of other business people they know. These contacts are called "Connections." A user can invite others whom they know to become a connection, and these contacts can be used to build up a network that will often grow exponentially through the connections of your contacts. The goal is to facilitate an introduction to someone you would like to meet through one of your trusted contacts. You can also use your connections to find jobs, other people, and business opportunities.

LinkedIn® gives you excellent control of searches by name, title, company and industry type, as well as any keyword of your choice. You can even sort your list under "Interest Level." And the possibilities include such designations as "hiring managers" and "potential employees."

LinkedIn® has a cost-free "core" level, but the service also offers three paid levels starting with their Business level at about $20 a month. You can add more search capability for either $50 per month for the Business Plus level or $200 per month for the Pro level. I would suggest starting with the free level. It will provide you with up to 100 names per search. You can search by any combination including location (zipcode), title, keyword, industry (general name) and other criteria.

Your results will include name, title, current company and city. Results do not include phone numbers and street addresses, but you can add these later with a quick Internet search. If LinkedIn® cannot provide a suitable list of names, then you'll want to move to one of the paid research sites listed below.

Spoke®

Describing itself as "Enterprise Software for Relationship Selling," Spoke® sells its ability to improve sales productivity by harnessing the power of relationships. Basically, Spoke® is online contact software designed for sales and business contacts.

The free level allows you to research people by name, job title, location, company, industry classification and other criteria to find names of some 40 million people within over 2.3 million companies. You are limited to a set number of searches per day; after that limit has been reached, the software closes out and you will not have access until 24 hours later, plus many names will remain inaccessible.

For $50 a month, you can upgrade to the premium level and have unlimited search capability. As with LinkedIn®, Spoke® has a large number of upper-level corporate managers and executives and is a particularly good tool for developing a list of names of potential hiring managers within target companies, since it provides very complete contact information, including phone numbers. The premium service may list e-mail addresses, as well. Spoke also has members in the lower echelons, even down to administrative assistant.

With Spoke® you can search for people by name, title and company. We advise investing in Spoke® Pro for at least a month or two while you perform your fundamental research. This will give you more in-depth search and reporting capabilities. For instance, an advanced search under Spoke® Pro would allow searches by location, metro area, industry type, company size, and revenue.

Although you can get much of this corporate info from other sources such as Hoovers® or Lead411®, these sources will not provide you with the names and titles of the mid- to lower-level managers, who are potentially your first contact points within any given organization. You'll be targeting individuals who have titles that would be potential hiring managers or decision-makers.

Look for job titles of people who might be your boss or your boss's boss (two levels up). With smaller companies, this could be a VP, but with most larger companies this would encompass titles such as Department Supervisor or Manager, Division Manager, Project Manager, etc., depending upon your particular expertise and the departmental structure and organization within each particular company. Try for as many titles as possible; you can always whittle the list down later.

ZoomInfo®

This is a vertical search engine that concentrates on the relationships between people and companies. ZoomInfo® builds its database from information extracted from websites by electronic "crawler" that reads certain information on websites and extracts information already on the Web. ZoomInfo® now offers users the ability to add or modify information. Not a social networking tool, this is a corporate research tool designed to be used by recruiters, salespeople and corporate researchers. *Side note: Advertising copy claims that the top ten recruiting firms and 20% of the Fortune 500 companies use ZoomInfo® to locate candidates.*

If you're currently (or have recently been) in a management role with a known company or a high level officer with a small firm, the chances are good you will be listed in ZoomInfo®. If you're in ZoomInfo®, you'll get noticed by recruiters more often.

Unfortunately, you can't put yourself in ZoomInfo®. You need to be "found" by the site's crawlers as they continually search for new information. While you are employed, you can enhance your chances of being found by being listed on your corporate site's management team or other internal pages. You could also enhance your visibility by writing position or technical papers and linking them to your corporate site or posting them on industry-related sites.

ZoomInfo® has several different levels of research capability:

Paycheck 911

1) The basic level is free and can be accessed to search over 37 million people, 3.5 million companies and jobs. You can search for companies, for people by name and for jobs by industry, company and position.

2) The ZoomExec level give access to profiles, including contact information, for 1.5 million executive-level contacts (including VPs, SVPs, GMs and c-levels). This costs $99/month.

3) ZoomInfo® PowerSearch and ZoomInfo® PowerSell are extra-cost, subscription-based options designed for recruiters or sales teams. At this level, the service will access profiles and contact information for 37 million people and 3.5 million companies.

You can use ZoomInfo® to search for jobs at the basic level. Search by title, industry, geography, or other basic job specifications. Unfortunately, ZoomInfo® at the free level is no longer appropriate for names research into companies. To make practical use of names research as described here, you'll need to invest in one of the above extra-cost service levels.

Since ZoomInfo® is considerably more expensive than Spoke®, we would consider using ZoomInfo® only as a third resort after LinkedIn® and Spoke®.

What the !!! is NAICS? And Why Should I Care?

The North American Industry Classification system (NAICS) and its predecessor, the Standard Industrial Classification (SIC), is a numbering system used to identify any company that produces a product or service. It's very similar to the system your library uses to classify each distinct book with a unique number. Before your eyes glaze over, be assured that this won't be an in-depth class on some arcane numbering system. You won't need to be concerned with all the ins and outs of NAICS. We'll only touch on the bare minimum so you can be merrily on your way.

NAICS is a six-digit numbering system generally designed to replace the former SIC codes. Used by the governments of the US,

Canada and Mexico to measure economic activity, you'll find this system useful when you're initially researching target companies.

Outside North America

The system used by other countries is similar to the NAICS and is called the International Standard Industrial Classification (ISIC) system. For a complete numbering breakdown of this system, you can visit the United Nations Statistical Division site at this page: http://unstats.un.org/unsd/cr/registry/regcst.asp?Cl=27.

I credit Wikipedia® with this example, as it clearly shows how this system works and how each added digit further focuses on a particular industry:

- Sector 33 = Manufacturing
- Subsector 339 = Miscellaneous Manufacturing
- Industry Group 3399 = Other Miscellaneous Manufacturing
- Industry 33994 = Office Supplies (except Paper) Manufacturing
- U. S. Industry 339941 = Pen and Mechanical Pencil Manufacturing

You can see how the numbers break down to differentiate each specific industry (Pen and Mechanical Pencil Manufacturing in this example).

We don't care what the numbers mean. We only care about how to use them to build our target company list to include all the similar companies that provide the same product or service.

NAICS and SIC NAICS are tools that you'll use to widen your target company list and open your eyes to companies you would previously have never known about. If your database is using the SIC or the ISIC system, the same mechanics of the below example apply. The system itself is unimportant. You only need it to look up and cross-check by that number.

Example:

Let's say you've identified the Ajax Pen Company in Irvine, California as one company you might like to work for because your skills would seem to fit well there. Knowing this, you go to a source such as Hoover's® and look up Ajax. You find they have the NAICS number 339941 (as above). Now you can do a cross-check and search for any other companies within the Irvine area (limit your search by zipcode) that might also have the same NAICS number of 339941. This is the way you'll build your initial target company list.

Begin with known companies; look up their NAICS. Then look up all the other companies that have the same number. Note: Search criteria in the various corporate databases allow you to limit your searches by state and/or zipcode so you won't have to weed out those companies that are geographically inaccessible to you. Most likely, you'll end up with some companies that you know and many others that you aren't aware of. For each of those companies, research them further through Hoover's®, EBSCO® or whatever library database you're using. Otherwise, use Lead411®.

You can also check out their corporate website to learn more about them. Remember, this is going to be your target list. Take care and time in building your list, as you will be marketing yourself to actual people in these companies.

The time spent now in this stage will pay rich rewards as you move into the marketing stage and send your Letters of Inquiry to the people who work and hold management positions within these companies.

Using Your Local Library to Widen and Improve Your Search

Want to take some control in your job search but don't know where to start? Have you thought of starting with your local public library?

General Library Resources and Databases

A library database is an online resource purchased by your local public library that offers access to full-text magazine and newspaper articles, abstracts, indices, and more.

Although library databases are typically free to use, most are not available outside the library unless they have been digitized and made accessible through the library's website.

The two major benefits of using library resources are that they are free to you as long as you have a library card that is valid in the library system you use. You can also access most of these online references from your computer at home, although you will first need a valid library card.

Most libraries have a well-stocked section of business references. The following references and databases are all found in the public library system in Phoenix, Arizona, USA. While your library may be different, this listing should be representative of resources you'll be able to find and use.

Associations Unlimited

Profiles of approximately 460,000 international and U.S. national, regional, state and local nonprofit membership organizations in all fields, including IRS data on U.S. 501(c) nonprofit organizations.

Business Directory - Reference USA

Database of more than 11 million U.S. companies can be searched by business name, type, size or location.

Business and Company Resource Center

Business and Company Resource Center is a fully integrated database bringing together company profiles, brand information, rankings, investment reports, company histories, chronologies, HR law case digests, and over 4,000 magazines, journals, and newsletters. The job seeker, researcher, or casual investor can find up-to-date company and industry information on thousands of global companies.

EBSCO® Business Source Complete

Full-text journal and non-journal content such as financial data, company profiles, SWOT analyses (strategic planning tool used to evaluate the Strengths, Weaknesses, Opportunities, and Threats), case studies and more can be found here.

Hoover's® Company Records

Find up-to-date records on more than 40,000 public and non-public U.S. and international companies and 225,000 key executives. Record may include: Fact sheet, overview, history, people, financials, products & operations, subsidiaries & affiliates, and competitors.

ThomasNet®/Thomas Register®

This is a very comprehensive resource for industrial information, products, services, CAD drawings, brand names and more. You can search by product or service name, brand name and company, plus sort by location (state or province).

Mergent Online®

Morningstar's data reports cover more than 20,000 securities, including both stocks and mutual funds.

EBSCO® Newspaper Source

EBSCO® Newspaper Source provides access to the full text of 26 television and radio news transcripts and 17 newswire and newspaper columns. Thirty U.S. national newspapers, more than 20 major international newspapers and 200 regional U.S. newspapers. Newspapers provide selected full text to business content. Sources include *CBS News, Chicago Tribune, Christian Science Monitor, CNN, FOX News, Knight Ridder Tribune, MSNBC, National Public Radio (NPR), New York Daily News, USA Today* and *The Washington Post*.

Standard & Poor's®Net Advantage

Stock reports providing data, analysis, recommendations and charts on over 5,500 publicly traded companies. Includes company profiles, executives, bonds, investment and economic news. Industry Surveys section offers overviews of 50+ industries.

How to Use the Want Ads
To Find Possible Hidden Jobs

And you thought the Want Ads were a waste of time!

How many times have you applied for a job in the Want Ads only to receive the *"Sorry, we'll keep your résumé on file"* form letter? Or to find out that you were one of hundreds of applicants?

Today, you'll learn an easy way to use CareerBuilder® or other Want Ads to tap into dozens of possible *HIDDEN JOBS* and find yourself in the enviable position of being *the only applicant* for the job you really want with no other competition!

This is simple. *Go where others don't go.* Just because a company is not listing a job this week or month that you would qualify for does not mean they don't need you and won't hire you. *Your goal is to find those companies who WERE hiring in the relatively recent past.*

Here's what you do: go back 30, 60, and 90 days to find the companies that listed jobs with your job title and skills (if the search capability allows this). You are doing this to be first in line when the company is ready to hire the *next* person with your skills. They could be getting ready to pull the trigger and begin a *new* search today or next week to:

- replace the person they just hired (and this happens more often than you think).
- fill a new position that was just budgeted.
- replace a person who was just promoted.

You have this capability online with the Careerbuilder® section of the newspapers. Unfortunately with Careerbuilder®, you can only go back a maximum of 30 days. An advantage with Careerbuilder® though, is that they give you a contact name to follow up with. Add this person's name to your "Follow-up today" list.

With other papers' online Want Ads, such as those in *The Arizona Republic*™, you can find listings as far as a year or more back.

Otherwise, go to the library and ask for help in retrieving this information for you. It may prove to be invaluable.

Don't overlook the trade papers such as *The Business Journal*™ or other local civic and trade-related papers in your city. They tend to focus on business developments, promotions, new hires and legal transactions, both corporate and civic. Pay attention to the sections on promotions and new hires. This may reap a reward with the attendant empty spot left open, or the need for another hire due to increased sales activity or department expansion. Get a contact name to follow up with.

Don't stop there. Do the same as above—go backwards 30, 60, and 90 days. You're getting valuable information about which companies are most likely to be in need of your services at any point in time. You are also getting a huge leg-up by building your list of names and titles for follow up purposes today as well as over the next several weeks.

Once again, the key to finding gold in the job search game is to go where others don't go and to do the things others don't think to do or know how to do.

List Providers—Buying Lists

A list provider is a vendor that maintains comprehensive databases of information on corporations that include locations, contact info, industry classification, employees, job titles/functions and a whole range of specialty data that include revenues, sales trends, tax info and so forth. These vendors make this information available on a fee basis to corporations and individuals, who may use the data in list form for sales prospecting or telemarketing purposes, or as specialized industry reports.

The major list provider we have found is a company called Zapdata®, an Internet service of D & B Sales and Marketing solutions. Dun & Bradstreet® is one of the pre-eminent providers of corporate data worldwide. As a result, Zapdata® can be used to cull data from over 80 million businesses, 14 million of which are U.S. companies. This is an alternative to looking up information directly from sources such as Hoover's®, EBSCO® and even D&B itself, then cross linking this with names and titles of decision-makers and managers.

You can custom design a specialty list from Zapdata® with all of the information on one list. This can be advantageous since you will save considerable time on your research once you know which industrial classifications you'll be targeting. You'll have a custom, consolidated list with only the companies and targeted individuals at the specific locations you requested. The downside is a slight increase in your cost versus paying the premium Spoke® or ZoomInfo® monthly fee to look up this information yourself. Your fee may range from $0.20 to $0.53 per lead depending on the size of your list.

Ordering a Custom Prospect List

I'll use Zapdata® as our example. Don't feel limited to this organization. There are many others who provide similar services and pricing that will likely be comparable. Use Google® keywords such as "mailing lists" or "sales leads" and you will uncover several other vendors, which include InfoUSA.com®, GoLeads.com®, SalesGenie.com®, and DirectMail.com®, to name a few.

Once you've entered the Zapdata® home page, you'll first need to create an account (no charge) and log into their system. Once into the operating pages, you can play around with the different criteria until you create a list. To create your list, you'll select "Prospect Lists." You'll be taken to a page where you will build your list in five steps:

1) Select your location(s)

You can choose everywhere or limit by state, city or metro area, county, or zipcode.

2) Select Industries

Remember those NAICS and SIC numbers? Here's where you'll use them. Zapdata® happens to use the older SIC numbering system, but that's of no concern. You can type in the industry and the software will guide you through the process of drilling down by the industries you choose and checking those you want to target.

3) Demographics

You can include or exclude by number of employees and annual sales volume.

4) Specialty Data

This is a section that can be used to add specialty data but you most likely won't need any of this, as it's mostly special sales prospecting data.

5) Job Function.

Here you'll want to choose specialty job function contacts beyond the top executives. Try to select the names of titles that would be one, but no more than two, levels above your position. With smaller companies, that may be a VP level person. The easiest approach is to select from the list and drill down on each title until you come to a detailed listing where you can check the most appropriate titles.

You'll be given a choice of several purchase options to actually order your list. You're never charged until you actually order specific data.

With Zapdata® there is an additional cost of about four cents per lead for specialty job function contacts. Once you complete your criteria selection, you can view the results where you'll be taken to a screen that shows the actual number of leads (names) on your list and the various data record options. With Zapdata®, there are five options with graduated costs for each.

For our purposes, we only need the second lowest cost option, called the "Telemarketing Record," which yields the business name, mailing address, city, state, zip+4, primary SIC, DUNS#, county, FIPS codes, D&B codes, MSA code/text, lat-lon coordinates, standard executive contact information (name, title, gender, executive function code), population code, carrier route code and delivery point, additional SIC codes (if available), plus any specialty data elements and contact names chosen, plus the telephone number.

Some of even this info you won't need. Yet it's an easy way to compile your search target list. As a gauge, plan on spending about $53 for 100 names, $160 for 500 names, and $200 for 1,000 names.

Your list may total any number, and you'll only be charged on a per name basis—and the larger your list, the lower the per name cost.

Once you have ordered and paid for your list, you are now ready to import the data into your database. You can extract the info on an individual basis, or you can set it up to run a mail merge into your Word software.

Keep in mind, if you are going to follow-up with these contacts, which I highly recommend, mail only a small number of letters at a time. This allows you time to make the calls to those prospects you've just mailed. You want your call to be timely. That means three to four days after they receive the letter.

The process at InfoUSA® is slightly different. The list of titles to choose from appears to be significantly fewer than with Zapdata®. For the particular list that I compiled, the pricing seemed a bit higher than for Zapdata®. InfoUSA® claims to verify all of their information by telephone, which may be a slight advantage.

Section IV -- MARKETING

In this section you will learn about making contact and developing relationships with company executives, professional recruiters and corporate Human Resources departments.

Making First Contact

The Letter of Introduction

Up to 80% of job hires do not come from Internet postings. They stem from referrals, hence the extreme importance of your Letter of Introduction.

What It Is

A letter of introduction (LOI) is your first point of contact with the outside world. Though some people might confuse this with a letter of qualifications, a letter of inquiry is a stand-alone marketing piece designed to attract *attention,* create *interest* in your achievement(s), and whet an employer's *desire* to know more about you.

Remember, you're looking for a qualified buyer for your talents. An LOI serves to pre-qualify your reader's interest in your achievements, and its true objective is to win a later phone conversation with your reader.

How You Will Use It

A letter of introduction is designed to be used *without a résumé* in situations where there is no specific job listed. Your goal is to establish initial contact with a potential hiring authority or manager within a company, someone with whom you want to explore employment opportunities. The content of the letter must generate interest in your achievements and imply that you can do the same for this company.

Here Are the Three Vitally Important Things You Are NOT Doing with This Letter:

- *You are not asking for a job*
- *You are not asking whether the company is hiring*
- *You are not asking for an interview*

Some authorities in job search will suggest that you include your résumé, but they miss the point. The LOI is intended to pave the way for your phone call, which you will make within a few business days of sending your letter.

Using the Letter of Introduction

Never send a generic letter. Always address it to an individual, by name, if at all possible. Never send this to HR (unless you're applying for a position in the HR department). You will put this letter in an envelope, address it, put a stamp on it and send it by way of your country's mail service.

Here are the reasons why you are going to do this:

- E-mail is considered SPAM, and if it's not already blocked by the corporate SPAM filters, it most assuredly will be deleted by your intended reader. Managers and execs probably receive 50 or more e-mails to every piece of correspondence that was physically mailed.

- Mail is usually distributed in the early part of the day and physically left somewhere on your target manager's desk waiting to be opened. There will be a curiosity element attached to your letter.

- The fact that you actually wrote, signed and mailed a letter to this one person by name sets you apart from the rest of your competitors. Your letter will most likely get opened and read. If you've included all the noted elements in as succinct and concise a manner as possible, you will most likely be remembered.

The Elements Your Letter of Introduction Should Contain

1. Always personalize the address

Do your research. Send it to a real person, not some title such as "Director of Engineering" or worse yet, the dreaded "to whom it may concern."

2. Introduce yourself with your USP or branding sentence

This can come straight from your exercise in developing your USP.

3. Tell them why you're writing

It needs no more than a few words such as, "I feel that my skills can further enhance your growth and accomplishments."

4. Flatter them

Explain why you're interested in this particular company (a specific reason). It may be general and you only need a few words at most. It could be about their product line, any recent news such as a new product introduction, or even a general comment such as "I have been impressed with your company's strong position in your market." Whatever you decide, be sure to include this sentence or phrase, ideally including the actual name of the company.

5. Add one or two solid but brief examples to back up your USP

These should be short benefit statements, preferably monetized, that you can cite from your current or previous employer.

6 Close

Let them know that you will follow up *by phone* within three to five business days.

On the following three pages are several sample letters for you to use as models.

Sample Letter of Introduction #1

Dear _____:

As a seasoned Director of Software Engineering, my strength in planning and execution of large Web-based solutions for the healthcare and telecom industries has saved my previous two employers 20% in development costs. After researching your organization, I am impressed with your accomplishments in *(specific example)*. I feel that my skills can further enhance your growth and accomplishments.

For example, while in my most recent position as Director of Software Engineering for Stratus, I was challenged to build, train and direct a strong team of developers and managers in a short period of time. Not only did I rise to the challenge and deliver a quality product on time, but we also cut development costs by $1 Million, a 50% reduction.

Previous to that, while at GE Medical Solutions, I helped save three months' development time by advocating Agile Software process with the development teams located overseas. This increased productivity by minimizing misdirection and communication latencies. This resulted in a savings of $500K.

I will contact you within the next five days to discuss ways that I might achieve similar results for your team. Should you have any questions before that time, please feel free to call me at 610-555-5669 or e-mail me at name@domain.com.

Thank you for your time and consideration.

Sincerely,

Samir Vankat

~ ~ ~

Sample Letter of Introduction #2

Dear _____:

As a seasoned Marketing Manager, I have additional strengths in both online and offline advertising that have resulted in $1.2 Million in added revenue for my employer in only six months' time. After researching your organization, I am impressed with your accomplishments in (YYY). I feel that my skills can further enhance your growth and accomplishments.

For example, while with the Selmer Group I was charged with creating and maintaining the daily operation of a new retail website for Rockway Shoes. I was able to increase Web sales from $300,000 to over $1.5 Million in less than six months for Selmer. While with Vantage, I created and implemented six new niche markets including one idea that increased the draw into our trade show booths by 150 percent.

I will contact you within the next five days to discuss ways that I might achieve similar results for your team. Should you have any questions before that time, please feel free to call me at (949) 555-9853 or e-mail me at name@domain.com

Thank you for your time and consideration.

Sincerely,

James Langford

~ ~ ~

Sample Letter of Introduction #3

Dear _____:

As a seasoned Project Manager, my strengths in identifying and solving problems have saved my employers over $10 Million while completing over $35 Million worth of projects during the past 9 years.

After researching your (company) organization, I am impressed with your accomplishments in (*). I feel that my skills can further enhance your company's bottom line, since my various roles are those of "Problem Solver", "Diplomat/Leader" and "Project Professional".

For example, while in my most recent position as Project Director for UltraTech, I provided key leadership to drive $31 Million worth of projects to finish on time and under budget. I achieved this with my ability to identify problems early.

I also saved a $17 Million investment in a prior project by winning over key staff to the project methodology.

I will contact you within the next five days to discuss ways that I might achieve similar results for your team. Should you have any questions before that time, please feel free to call me at 801-555-9324 or e-mail me at name@domain.com

Thank you for your time and consideration.

Sincerely,

Calvin Firestone, MBA, PMP

How to Develop
A Working Relationship
With a Recruiter

As a job hunter, you'll probably seek out the services of a recruiter (or headhunter)—and why not? Recruiters can be a good source of hidden opportunities and can lobby on your behalf to their clients.

As a recruiter, I've spent the past 15 years finding and placing top candidates in some of the best jobs of their careers. I'm also known on the Internet as "The Job Search Guy." I have received hundreds of questions from job seekers asking me how to work effectively with recruiters.

Recruiters Can Be Helpful

Here are six guidelines for working with recruiters that can help you make the best use of recruiting agencies in your job search.

1. Recruiters Are Businesspeople

Recruiters work for the client who pays their fee. A recruiter is *not* your guidance counselor, career coach, therapist or mother. A recruiter does *not* work for you. All conversations that take place with candidates are done so with the intention that a fee can be received on an eventual placement. Before talking with any recruiter, do your homework. Do not talk with a recruiter with the expectation that it's his or her job to find you a position.

2. Don't Waste Your Time (*or theirs*)

Have *your* act together. Then look for recruiters who have *their* act together. As with your résumé, you should be focused and know exactly what it is you are looking for and the benefits you provide to an employer. Then, look for recruiters who specialize in your particular industry or specialty niche. Not all recruiters have current search assignments that you might match. Many don't work in your specialty area. Focus on only those agencies or independent recruiters who understand your business, profession or industry, and who regularly place people with your skills and talents.

Call and ask to speak briefly with the person who specializes in your career area. Describe who you are, what specific experience you bring and what position(s) you are looking for. State your USP. Then ask if they are currently working with client companies who could use someone with your particular skills or background. They either do or don't. Listen for their answer to this question and if they appear vague, thank them and move on. Don't waste your time.

3. Hold onto That Résumé

Have your résumé ready, but avoid blindly sending it to a recruiter or recruiting firm without first talking face-to-face (or at least over the phone) with someone at the target firm. Once you've sent your résumé, you no longer have leverage or power. They have your information, so there is little reason for them to talk with you.

4. They Must Get Your OK Before Submitting Your Résumé

Once you and a recruiter have agreed to work together, it is imperative that you take this action:

*Indicate upfront that you must be consulted about any opportunity **before** they send your résumé **anywhere**.*

You don't want your résumé sent to any employer without your knowledge. It is not at all uncommon for a candidate to have their résumé end up *at his or her own company*. That can be more than just embarrassing.

5. Keep Your References to Yourself

Although you may be asked to sign paperwork giving them permission to perform background and reference checks, never give references up front. As with employers, no reputable recruiter needs to know names and phone numbers of your references, unless a job offer is imminent. By the way, this is an old trick in the staffing industry. Less ethical recruiters use this strategy as an easy way to get fresh leads. They will source your references and get *their* résumés. Often, these recruiters are not even interested in *you*. They want the names of your bosses and co-workers. If they insist on playing this game with you, politely end the conversation.

6. What If a Recruiter Calls You First?

This may be a surprise, but the really good recruiters don't use sources such as Monster® to find candidates for their search assignments. They look for passive candidates—those who aren't looking. Should a recruiter call you, you have a right to know how they acquired your name. The recruiter should give the source, unless the referral was given with the exclusive requirement to not reveal same. If this is a problem, then you can disengage from further conversation.

Recruiting firms can be a good source of job opportunities, and they can also be good lobbyists for you. However, you must be vigilant because not all recruiters are equal. You deserve to work with only the best. Once you know your rights and responsibilities, you can develop a good working relationship with a professional recruiter who can be a good resource for your job search.

Dealing Effectively with Human Resources

Avoid Being a Lemming

Doesn't the term "human resources" have a deceptively nice ring to it? It conjures up images of generous, helpful administrators eagerly conducting matchmaking services between wannabe employees—such as you—and harried hiring managers, totally overwhelmed with hundreds of résumés for one job. Unfortunately, in most cases, nothing could be further from the truth.

The fact is, human resources personnel are not paid to be your friends. Their job isn't to open doors of opportunity for you. Frankly, most of them don't care a twit about you. They're paid to process thousands of résumés that are entered into their company's databases through such sources as Internet ads, the company's websites, job fairs and goldmines such as Monster® and Careerbuilder®.

The goal of human resources is not to find the best, brightest or most qualified candidate for an opening. Rather, HR is more about maintaining its own domain (whether functional or dysfunctional) within the corporation. It's about protecting their turf and perpetuating their own authority or fiefdom within the organization. To do this, they've created a dysfunctional system where all funnels must go through them.

Many human resources departments employ contract recruiters. These are individuals hired on a contract basis to recruit for specific job openings. They also fish the Internet and job fair waters for résumés that they often add to their own private résumé databases. When many of these contract recruiters leave to take contract recruiting jobs with other companies, they take this database of résumés. It's not uncommon for both HR personnel and contract recruiters to "source" the résumé owners for the names of other candidates.

Additionally, a human resources manager wears many hats. That person's responsibilities are not limited to hiring new employees. Their duties include dealing with issues such as employee benefits and compensation, employee assistance programs, diversity programs, employee training, and complying with numerous government reporting programs involving affirmative action and statistics on the company's hiring practices. The truth is, the hiring process is a system set up to keep the system itself thriving, not you.

Face it. You are just a piece of paper to someone in human resources. It would be counter to our message to instruct you on how to play their game. It would consist of how to put the proper keywords onto your résumé, how to get past indifferent, sometimes hostile human resource personnel. And how to ingratiate yourself to get your résumé placed in the short pile, etc.

Instead, our message is that playing by traditional rules of job search will not get you the job you want. We encourage you to *break the traditional good boy/good girl behavior of job search* to leap past human resources and everything that they represent.

A successful job search involves innovation, not playing "by the book." It requires creativity, not mind-numbing, half-committed attempts to find a job by going through the process that others (mainly human resource directors and managers) have dictated to the masses in order to hire people on their terms.

If you really want to succeed—to take a different direction from the job hunting lemmings who leap when they're told to leap, turn when told to turn, speak up when prompted, shut up when directed, and place their job search in the hands of authority figures—don't even consider talking to human resources personnel.

The best recruiters in the business refuse to work with human resources. They expect and achieve direct contact with the hiring managers in order to find and place top-notch candidates in hard-to-fill openings. *Why shouldn't you also expect to deal directly with a hiring manager, at least during critical initial aspects of your job search process?*

Human resources should not dictate your career path. You are in charge of your search process. The sooner you own this process, the sooner you'll be successful. We are encouraging you to own the process from the beginning. Don't turn it over to the HR staff. It's your employment future that's at stake, not theirs. No one can possibly care about your job search more than you do. The buck stops with you, it also starts with you.

Our advice is to avoid dealing with human resources, at least during the early stages of your contact with a company. See them as hurdles to jump over, effortlessly, as you achieve your job search goals.

Are You a "Job Seeker" or a "Job Hunter?"

If you aren't in the human loop, you are forever locked into playing the game of outsider always looking in. You're trying to shove your résumé into the "In Box" to be intercepted by some HR admin type and buried along with the résumés of hundreds, if not thousands, of other lost souls. This is the endless fate of most job seekers.

After all, the Internet and the job search industry still sells this idea that job search is as easy as booking a hotel or a flight on Priceline®. They promote this fallacy because they want to be in control. They don't want to be overrun by the advancing Mongol hordes, so they set up all these barriers and hoops to jump through.

Most job seekers gladly comply, take a number, and wait in line. When it starts to dawn on you, the job seeker, that this is *your career and your life*, then you'll end your complacency and start playing a new game—the game of becoming a ***job hunter***.

To move from job *seeker* to job *hunter* requires concerted work. Job *seekers* are passive "point and clickers." They've become addicted to sending their résumé to Monster® and all the usual job posting watering holes and then sitting back and waiting, hoping their prey will venture into their lap by virtue of a phone call. Contrary to the advertising, that's neither a fun nor empowering process.

A job *hunter*, on the other hand, will go out and actively entice his quarry (with a letter of introduction) and be armed and ready for a response. To evolve into a job *hunter* means getting into the muck of putting yourself out there, taking a small chance and actually developing a conversation with someone you most likely don't know.

Consider this: résumés don't win interviews. It's the conversation that wins the interview. In fact, it's the conversation that wins the job. A résumé may open the door, but it's always the conversation (phone screen) that wins the actual interview. The reason is that people hire people. They don't hire pieces of paper. They want to know about that person before they will commit to them as a possible coworker.

An employer's first choice is to interview and hire people they already know. When that's not possible, they interview referrals from people they know. When a hire from the inside is not possible, their last choice is to interview strangers off the street who may have submitted their résumé online.

Job search remains a human, high-touch process and will always be so. People like to hire people they know and feel comfortable with. That doesn't mean hiring managers hire their best friends and acquaintances, but it does mean that they almost always prefer to hire people they either know directly or who were referred by someone they know (and trust).

Since it's likely that you don't have a large Rolodex or a hefty network in place, you need an "in" that can put you in the loop with a company that you target. That's why you're targeting individuals who work at the companies you chose. You'll first send them your marketing piece—the letter of introduction covered earlier—briefly explaining why you're writing and the biggest benefit you offer to this company. This sets the stage for step two, your follow-up phone call.

Phone Presentation

The purpose of a phone presentation is to engage in a conversation with a company insider. This person may or may not be a hiring manager. It doesn't matter because being an insider, they have information and that information can be very helpful to you in your job hunt. They also have the power to refer you to another decision-maker within the company. If you've done your job well, that person won't be HR.

You *could* avoid this stage. You *could* send a standard letter of introduction along with your résumé and then sit back and wait—but you won't get the conversation with these people. You won't get the leads and the inside information. You won't develop any relationship with any of these people. In short, you will miss out on a large number of potential opportunities by not tantalizing them with your short letter and calling them a few days later.

Why Do *I* Need to Call *Them*?

When we say that job search is marketing, this is not some empty phrase. This implies a total shift *away* from the traditional passive *job seeker* approach of merely sending your résumé and waiting for someone to call you. Marketing means finding a customer or a user of your talents. The *job hunter* approach is going to consist of a one-two punch that very few, if any, of your competitors are doing. The first stage is your direct marketing piece—your Letter of Inquiry, which we have already discussed and illustrated, and the second stage is your *personal follow-up* by telephone.

The act of actually picking up the telephone and calling someone you don't know can seem terrifying to you, if you've never done this before.

Assuming your targets have read the letter (and there is a good chance of that), they will have some familiarity with whom you are and will probably remember at least a little bit about you and your branding USP statement.

The importance of this phone follow-up can't be overstated. Contacting people by phone has a much higher rate of success because *fewer people do it*. This initiative action on your part demonstrates that you've done all of your homework and are sincere and determined. It separates you from the pack, which is what you should strive to accomplish throughout your job search.

Remember, it doesn't matter what you can do or how good you are at what you do. **What matters is *how well you communicate* what you do**.

Phone follow-up separates you from the masses, making you more noticeable, and even more importantly, it also gives you an opportunity to tell a prospective employer what you do and how good you are.

As you've already learned, the "buyer's market" approach puts you in a one-down position. You cater to someone else's process, which can be dysfunctional to start with. You dance to their tune and you have little leeway. The more positive and assertive "seller's market" approach—the process we are discussing here—puts *you* in control. Yes, it requires that you get in the muck and get your hands dirty by making the first moves and by displaying a little "courage." And yes, you will put forth more research and self-packaging effort. But the results will almost certainly be more rewarding.

Ideally, you will create your own position! At the very least, you will have timed your contact so that you are on their doorstep solving their problem before that problem becomes a crisis. This is especially important because no manager wants to face and have to overcome difficult situations, particularly when they're centered around people. A hiring crisis will cause management to spring into action with a job requirement and ad, involving HR and the whole bureaucracy, which will throw you, and every other potential candidate, into a buyer's market. Don't let that happen.

Let's move forward now and talk about what that phone call should be like.

Your Initial Phone Call

Your phone call is a "high touch" part of your job search, the factor that separates you from all other "job seekers." It demonstrates that you know who you are, what benefits you offer, that you've done your homework, and that you're serious about your career. It's what gets you the conversation with a corporate insider.

Here's something important for you to chew on. Although your phone follow up to your Letter of Introduction is, in a way, a "first contact," it's not actually a "cold call" because your Letter of Introduction has provided a very strong introduction. You've told briefly why you were making contact and why you're interested in their company. You also described yourself with your USP and backed that up with one or two brief accomplishments that have benefited your current employer.

Oh, and you did one more thing. You promised them that you'd follow up by phone in a few days. *That makes this a "warm call."* Depending on the person's situation and workload needs, it could be a *very* warm call, and that's good for you.

You may have trouble believing this, but most business people read the mail that's delivered to their desk. There's a very good chance they will have read yours, and your letter was designed to make a favorable impression. It wasn't braggy, tacky or over the top; it was simple, straightforward and brief. If this person read your letter, it will remain in the recipient's memory for the few days until you call. Of course, you should never expect the recipient to call you.

But if that happens (and it sometimes does), rejoice. It means they've seen something in your communication that they need *now!*

By the same token, don't wait two weeks to follow-up. Not only will they have most certainly forgotten you by then, but even worse, you will have left a promise (to call them in three to five days) unfulfilled—and they probably *will* remember that (unfavorably to you).

It's also possible that they did not read, or have forgotten, your letter, but even then you won't lose all the advantage because there you are, on the line, and you should be prepared to tell them exactly what your letter said you had done in the past and could do for them in the future. At the very least, if the party on the other end of the phone pleads "too busy to talk now," you can offer to re-send the letter, then repeat the follow up call in another three days or so. We guarantee that if that happens, you will be remembered (favorably).

Regardless of the actual course of the call, remember that you must be clear in your mind about your primary objective. You want one of three outcomes.

1. You want to set up a face-to-face meeting where you will talk further . . . or
2. You want to set up a time to talk more in depth on the phone with either this person or with another decision-maker . . . or
3. You want to get the name and contact information of someone else who may have an employment opportunity either open or forthcoming within the company.

While the chances of outcome 1 (an interview) happening might seem remote, don't discount it entirely. However, it's more likely that either outcomes 2 or 3 will occur. Consider yourself "a winner" when any one of those occurs.

The Conversation Itself

When you're on the phone, paint a brief picture of yourself. You'll want to state clearly your Unique Selling Proposition (USP). This is what separates you from your competition. You should have only one or two sentences that are ready-made to describe yourself and your accomplishments. Take them from your letter and be ready to enlarge upon them, should you be asked. Remember, these people are busy, yet they are open to being tantalized—so tantalize them. You want to say just enough to get them to ask questions.

Remember the A.I.D.A. formula we discussed earlier? This is the Desire point. If you can get them to want to know more, you know you've already won some positive outcome. After that, you'll close (ask) for outcome 1, 2, or 3 above.

Let's cover this conversation in easy pieces.

First, introduce yourself and ask permission for their time. It can go like this:

> "Hi, Mr. Roberts. My name is Christine Talbot. I believe you received my short letter of introduction a few days ago."

He'll either say "yes" or "no, I don't remember."

If he says "no," offer to resend the letter and ask for his correct address.

If he wants to know more now, proceed as if he answered "yes" to your question.

Start with your biggest bang, your USP:

> "I'm a seasoned Financial Controller whose strengths in both P&L/balance sheet analysis plus financial modeling have been able to save my previous two employers $57 million over the past 7 years."

Now reconfirm his or her willingness to talk for a few minutes; this is a true courtesy that will not go unrecognized:

> "Did I catch you at a good time (or, do you have a few minutes to talk now)?"

Always show respect for their time. If you ask, they will almost always give you the green light for at least a few minutes of phone time.

Now get into a little detail about your potential value to the hiring company:

"After researching your company, I'm impressed with the fact that you recently added pork rinds to your impressive product array. I especially feel that my skills can further enhance your growth in this area. For example, while at Morgan Stanley, I revamped the allocation process and improved the cost allocation accuracy. This gave businesses added transparency into their costs. It also created an on-demand model that allowed for better pricing, versus purchasing it directly."

Well, that should get some interest. Obviously, you need to structure your USP in terms of your own past performance.

"The reason I'm calling, Mr. Roberts, is that I am looking for a new opportunity, and from my research on your company, I feel there might be some mutual areas of interest where we might talk.

Personalize every conversation by making it a point to use their name. None of us ever gets tired of hearing our name spoken. You want to generate enough interest on their part to desire *more information about yourself.*

If they answer in the affirmative and ask further questions about your background, you already have their *attention* and *interest*, and now you've stimulated their *desire* to know more.

The contact may ask a number of questions. This is good because each new question is, in a way, a *buying signal*. Learn to recognize this signal. It usually comes as a request for more information on your specific background, such as, "How many years of experience do you have?" or, "What particular financial models have you been using?" or "What's your formal education?" These questions indicate an interest in your experience and a need to find out more about you.

Get enough of these, and you are ready for the final closing question:

"Would it make more sense to arrange a face-to-face meeting now, or would you prefer to schedule another phone call when we might have more time for a conversation?"

Don't use the word "interview." It may carry too much baggage. Use less threatening terms such as "meeting" or "a time to get together." At this point, they will either agree to one of the above options, or they might refer you to another more appropriate contact to approach (a lead).

Or they may say they are not interested in pursuing further talks at this time. If this is the case, politely ask if there is someone else in the company who might be hiring, and if they would object to your following up with that person at a later date. Of course, they may volunteer this info, but once again, the onus is on you to come away with one of the three objectives we set forth a few pages ago:

- A face-to-face meeting (interview) where you will talk further
- A time to talk more in-depth on the phone with either this person or another decision-maker
- A lead (name) to someone else who may have an opportunity within the company, or with another company

Even if the answer is "no," it should be possible most of the time to achieve one of the first three objectives. They might still have a lead for you, or they might be open to future discussions (so it's just a timing issue).

There is always the possibility that you will be referred to HR. If this happens, it's important to ask these two questions:

"Is there an opening for (the target position) that you know about?"

If the answer is positive, say this:

"I'll be happy to follow up with HR. Do you know who the hiring manager for this position will be?"

What makes this strategy so powerful? And why on earth would a perfect stranger ever want to answer leading questions like these?

People usually want to help other people. All you have to do is ask. After all, you just had a conversation with someone who is a likely fountain of information about the industry and who now knows a little about your background.

Know this: the person you are talking to has, in effect, turned you down even though that person has given you added, perhaps vital, information. He or she wants to end the conversation on a positive note, so take advantage of your position in this game and your knowledge of human nature.

Don't try to memorize these questions. Write them down! Make them your own by putting them into your own words. Then pick the one or two that you feel the most comfortable with. Write these down as part of your phone script and keep the others handy so that you can play your game, if you feel like it, when you're on the phone.

After you've done this a few times and feel more comfortable with the on-the-phone relationship, commit them to memory. You'll be amazed at the amount of support you get when you just ask.

When you get a lead, thank them, and always ask if you may use their name when you call to speak to the lead.

If, when you talk with the HR Department, you run into a gatekeeper, such as an overly ambitious administrative assistant who asks the nature of the business, simply say:

> "I recently mailed Mr. Roberts a letter regarding a sales (or accounting, or whatever your profession is) matter. He's expecting a follow-up call from me. Would you put me through, please?"

Shore up Your Network

Are you looking for a new or better job right now? If so, you should be familiar with the term "networking." Why? Because most jobs are filled from the inside through personal "word-of-mouth" referrals. Referrals can be the gateway to that 80% job market we've already referred to as "hidden." This means hiring people who employers already know as a referral from managers, employees, professional organizations, and any other connections that might have the ear of an insider.

Referrals are effective for companies because they produce better candidates and the cost is minimal. By contrast, a good recruiter will cost upwards of $20,000 for a quality placement. It's no wonder that a company's first choice in making a hire will be by first asking the question, "Who do we know?"

Network Now

The power of using the "grapevine" can't be overstated, yet most of us think of network-building as the plague. The very word "networking" sounds so business-like that it may stifle more than a few of you.

If this is the case, try thinking of networking as just another extension of relationship-building. Think of it as making some new friends. No pressure to perform, just having fun.

With that in mind, here are five action areas to help you take full advantage of your personal and professional networks:

1. Make a List of People You Already Know

Make a list of friends, colleagues and neighbors you haven't seen for a while. Go through your list of contacts and pick out five to ten to reconnect with. These individuals should be people you haven't seen in the past six months to a year or more.

E-mail is OK for these people, but if your relationship was solid, why not call them?

Be honest and up front about your situation. Ask permission to use them as a reference when the time comes. Assuming they say "of course," take it a step further. Tell them about your search. Explain to them what kind of opportunity you're searching for and ask them to keep their eyes and ears open for anything they might hear about.

As usual, follow up with a thank you note, then follow up every couple of weeks to ask about potential opportunities, any hiring that might be taking place and who is doing so.

Ideally, you want the name of a hiring manager, someone on the inside. It's important that you foster a relationship with as many contacts as you feel comfortable with, and then go a little further. Ask if they've heard of any companies that are hiring. If they can come up with a name within the company, that's great! Otherwise, the name of a company may be all you need to get your first break.

Should someone give you a name to call, *get permission to use your referrer's name, if possible.* Maintain contact. Follow up periodically. Thank them for any assistance. When you do get a job, let them know. Stay in touch periodically afterwards, since you never know when you might need their help again. Also, when you might be called upon to return a favor.

2. Uncover Networking Events You Can Attend

There are probably one or two networking events you can identify from your local newspaper that you can attend this month. Check out an association in your field; investigate the many business groups available. Check out your local trade or throwaway papers for events listed. Try the local *Business Journal*™'s Top 25 list, if that exists in your city. You can find the latest copy in your library.

Research the lists of associations and professional networks in your local area. Call them and find out the date and time of their next meeting and ask if you might attend. Get there early enough to spend some time mingling before the speaker starts. Push yourself a bit and spend some of your time there with people you don't know.

Although it may feel more comfortable to want to hang with just your gender, introduce yourself to people of both genders at these events. You may not be a member of this particular organization but you do have connections and experience to share. It's natural to feel uncomfortable at first, but be assured, many others who are there are going to be a bit uncomfortable as well.

3. Social Events on Your Calendar?

You may already have several social events lined up on your calendar. It could be your spouse's company picnic, an after-hours party or church mixer. Have a brief conversation with a few new people. A word of caution: these are social occasions. This is not the time to pass out a business card. That's a networking no-no, anyway. Go there to meet new people and be open to the possibilities that can develop later. Keep your résumé at home and just be open to making one new friend.

4. Are You a Member of a Professional Association?

Almost all industries, trades and professions have at least one professional organization that represents the profession, fosters a high standard level and explores new developments that might define or affect the industry or profession's future. You may already be a member of one or more associations related to your profession. In addition to having constant contact with others in your field, you'll quickly learn who your local players are.

Often there is some newsletter or website that you'll have access to. Some will include a special section for their members that lists "Jobs Available" and "Jobs Wanted." An added benefit to membership is that you receive access to a current directory of names and contact information. You can use this as a starting point to make direct inquiries about opportunities that might be open in your area. You already have the professional connection as well as being an association member.

Introduce yourself, outline your biggest strengths (USP would work great here) and then ask if they might have any information about current opportunities and developments that could result in an opportunity. To check out possible associations, you may want to review a resource called "Associations Unlimited," which profiles approximately 460,000 international and U.S. national, regional, state, and local nonprofit membership organizations in all fields. Find it in your library, or possibly access it online with your library card.

5. Are You a College Alumnus?

Most of us graduate from college with our degree and move straight to the work world, leaving our college days behind. This can be a big mistake, as most schools have an alumni association. In fact, if you went to a major college or university and you live in or near a large metro area, the chances are good that there is an active alumni organization in your own backyard. Usually social in nature, these chapters will often get together on a regular basis throughout the year, and it may be a good way to make new connections with other graduates.

Check with the Alumni Office of your school to see what activities and services it provides. Join the alumni organization and investigate their resources. Many alumni seek other alumni when they need to hire for their own company or organization. These members are aware of opportunities and could be open to connecting with a fellow alum, but you have to get yourself in the loop first.

Finally, don't forget *other job hunters.* Look for support groups already set up in your area that might be beneficial. Think of churches, community centers and corporate outplacement services. What about online? Do an online seach for company groups such as ex-IBM.com groups, for example. (http://groups.google.com)

Golden Rule of Networking: "Give Rather than Take"

Typical networking goes something like this: *"Hi, My name is _____. What do you do?"* And then it's off to the races with the "Big Sell" and handing out business cards. No wonder networking has a bad image.

Instead, do this. Introduce yourself. Have a low-key chat asking questions about the other person. If there seems to be a chemistry, look for ways that you can give before you take. Why not follow up by sending your conversational partner an interesting article or pass on a piece of helpful information? You'll be surprised at how little gestures like this will make their way back to you.

More on Social Networking Sites

Social networking sites represent a fairly new development on both the recruiting and the job search scenes. This is sophisticated software that provides its members a convenient way to find colleagues of specific background and to network online.

Social software is changing the way executive recruiting is conducted. It also has the capacity to change the way online job hunting can operate. This makes use of the number one maxim that we already know: "People prefer to hire (and work for) people that they already know."

Typically, social software networks operate on the principle that when you join, you can invite your contacts to join, too. The governing principle is that persons of influence will be selective about passing along references.

You can use social software in two ways.

One way is to stay within the network to make direct contact with individuals that you wish to target (such as hiring managers) by way of intermediary contacts. We examined that possibility earlier. And of course, the more contacts you have, the more connections you can make. This is especially true with both LinkedIn® and Facebook®, each of which has grown exponentially over the past two years.

The second way is to use people you know as "leverage" to contact people *they* know but *you do not*. This approach is less direct but often quite effective and can be measured in "degrees of separation."

First degree = you make connections within your own immediate circle.

Second degree = you can extend your range to include a connection through a friend of one of your friends.

Third degree = you can reach further out and attempt a contact with the friend of one of those friends.

Chances become much less effective at the 3rd degree level, so it's usually best to build your own core network with people you truly know and trust—but don't ever overlook the "degree" channel; it might be just what you need to make the "right" connection.

Let's look at the first way to use this network: to find people you already know, either inside or outside of LinkedIn®, and invite them into your network. It's always efficient to deepen your primary contacts in social networking situations.

Later on, as you look up managers and decision-makers from companies you'd like to work at, you may notice that contacts within your network, or friends they know, may have connections with the people you'd like to contact. You can send off a request for introduction through your network, and if the connections are strong, you may well gain an inside connection through your "first degree" friend and eventually develop a direct e-mail connection with this "second degree" or even "third degree" person.

One of the downsides of the LinkedIn® approach is, as more and more people see the benefit of establishing a personal network, invitations are being sent to people with whom they have only a slight acquaintance.

You can also use this network as a huge source to locate people and titles within any particular company or organization.

See the earlier section, *Researching the Hidden Job Market*. This use alone is worth its price many times over (*and it's free!*).

You'll soon find social networking to be an indispensable and powerful tool, greatly enhancing your search. With its ability to locate the names and titles of actual contacts—employees, project leaders, hiring managers—within virtually any company you choose, you'll soon have a good sized, focused list of *relevant* contacts that you can now call and speak with.

There are other networking sites, including Ryze.net®, Tribe®, and Spoke®, to name just a few. They don't yet have the user numbers or business usefulness of LinkedIn®. As mentioned earlier, both Facebook® and Myspace® have huge potential for possible business networking possibilities. Right now, the big game in town remains LinkedIn®.

Summary

When you build your network, you increase your chances of locating and winning the inside track to hidden jobs. Don't always expect your contacts to put you in touch with hiring managers who have specific job opportunities you may match. This rarely happens.

Remember: People know other people. As you tend to your network, you'll notice rewards in the form of inside information or a dynamite referral that can get you an inside track to the job you would love to win.

Section V --
INTERVIEWING

In this section we will cover the often subtle details of various types of interviews and how you can retain control and improve your outcomes even in the most intimidating of situations.

The Informational Interview

An Old Tool for a New Age: Sue's Story

I've survived several career changes, and one of my most effective tools was the informational interview.

During my first career change, I wanted desperately to leave drug and alcohol counseling for something that paid better and was less emotionally draining. Frankly, anything would have paid better and been less emotionally draining.

During my second career change, I left vocational rehabilitation counseling for the corporate world of recruiting. My challenge was leaving the social work arena for the business world. I wasn't going to buck the odds by taking a traditional approach to job search. Without the informational interview, my career change efforts would have sunk like the Titanic.

Dust Off This Old Workhorse
(*No, not me . . . the Informational Interview*)

This form of interview has probably been around since *before* the Titanic, and is particularly effective for new grads who are trying to land their first professional job. It's also a tremendous tool for career changers with transferable skills but who don't know much about other occupations and industries.

The beauty of the informational interview is that you, the job hunter, initiate it, and you can confidently state to the person you wish to interview that your meeting will have nothing directly to do with your job search: you are only seeking information about the industry, the opportunities (in a general sense), and the job market in your targeted executive's sphere of knowledge and interest.

The informational interview is a powerful sales tool because if you were to pick up the telephone today and call a stranger to ask whether he's hiring, the answer would likely be a resounding "no" followed by a quick hang up. The informational interview lets you discover and investigate those "hidden" jobs.

Getting Your Foot in the Door

An informational interview can provide you with a great opportunity to meet, in person, in the office of a potential hiring manager, make a good impression, pick her brains about her job and industry, and walk out with several new leads without turning her off with the words, "Are you hiring?"

Dirty Secret

The dirty secret of the job search industry is that most jobs are never advertised, in spite of the explosion of online job boards. Isn't it ironic that with all of the advances in Internet technology, most jobs are still filled informally by word of mouth? Some things never change. Just a fraction of job openings get posted and many aren't even formally developed into jobs when they're filled. You want to hear about jobs before they've been written up into job descriptions with a list of requirements. You don't want the HR department getting involved, because when they do, it means red tape and posting on Internet job boards and on the company's website. Just what you need—several hundred other résumés piled on top of yours!

Entering Job Search Hell Waving a Paper Fan

Trust me, you don't want to apply for a job opening at this stage of its development. The odds are heavily stacked against you. Hiring managers and human resource personnel are typically overwhelmed with huge numbers of résumés in response to their online ads and website postings. They've created a paper monster, and it'll eat you up.

Fact: It's easier for an employer to fill a job with someone familiar than to go through a complicated, expensive and often overwhelming hiring process. Some companies even pay their employees for leads that result in a hire. So it's best to separate yourself from the pack of job seekers, and become proactive. Your goal is to create a killer network and become an insider.

How to Conduct an Informational Interview

Start by doing your research. Use the Internet, newspaper and magazine articles, television programs, business publications, and other information sources to identify a list of jobs that potentially interest you.

Commit to networking and cold calling people, and ask everyone you meet for several more contacts. Follow this path of networking to develop a large number of contacts who will lead you to the hidden job opportunities that other job seekers—who only answer ads, won't ever know about.

Start with a notebook, a pen, and the telephone. Create a short script that introduces you, explains the purpose of your call, an interest in exploring the listener's occupation and industry, and requests a brief meeting of 30 minutes at their office. Take notes while on the phone.

Schedule a time to meet in person. Give the individual a choice of two days (called a forced choice), and when they've selected a day, offer a choice of times on their preferred date. You might ask, "Would Tuesday or Thursday work better for you?" "Would 10:00 am or 2:00 pm work better for you?"

At the Interview . . .

Bring your notebook, your pen and your résumé. Ask for your interviewer's business card. Ask for feedback on the résumé. Bring a list of questions about the individual's company, position, industry and opportunities in his or her field. This is all very valid inquiry in an informational setting; after all, you've come there to learn.

If an opportunity arises for you to present your résumé to your interviewer, do so, and ask for feedback. Most interviewers will have something to tell you, and it could be valuable later.

Once your qualifications are on the table, you can feel quite free to inquire about whether your interviewer is aware of any good opportunities, either within their company or in other companies.

In any event, try to leave that interview with at least three names of people to contact—and ask full information on each person; name and title, company, phone number, and even e-mail address. In this way, you will grow your contacts and travel through an ever-expanding informal network. Make sure to leave your contact information in the event that the individual may hear of a job lead that could interest you.

Use the contact information on your interviewer's business card to follow up with a hand written thank you note. Include your e-mail address and telephone number in that note.

By mastering the informational interview you can break away from the pack very quickly, and—in a completely non-threatening way—network your way to those hidden jobs. On your way you'll receive a heck of an education, easily and for free, that'll guide your search to the right career and job for you.

The Nuts and Bolts of Informational Interviews

It's been said that one out of every 200+ résumés leads to a job offer, yet it's been firmly established that one out of every twelve informational interviews leads to a job offer. What's amazing about these statistics is that *the focus of an informational interview is to gather information, not to ask for a job*. The message here is that this easy-to-accomplish strategy provides a better path to job offers than simply submitting a résumé to a company.

Here's why the informational interview is such a powerful employment tool. It takes you out of the lemming job search mode of conducting your search "by the book" with the masses. It allows you to learn about the companies and careers of potential hiring managers, build your confidence, clarify what is involved in a job before committing to it, gather new job leads and build your network of contacts. And, most importantly, you're accomplishing all of the above while your interviewer's guard is down. What a deal!

Four Simple Steps to Creating Informational Interviews And Building Networks

1. Develop lists of contacts and leads

Create a list of all of the people you already know including family, friends, neighbors, church members, mentors, teachers, social acquaintances, sports teammates, and friends, relatives and acquaintances of the above.

Add members of professional organizations and both online and offline social networking groups. Also, develop lists of contacts from sources such as Lead411®. There is a monthly charge for this service, which enables you to research companies in a given industry and develop the names and contact information for the upper management.

2. Request the interview

Request to meet in person. You can make this request through a phone call, e-mail note or traditional letter. If you e-mail or write a letter, follow up with a phone call. When you communicate with the hiring manager, indicate that you're not seeking a job, but rather that you're gathering information. Asking about job opportunities will turn off the listener, making it difficult to move forward with this person.

If you received the hiring manager's name from a mutual contact, be sure to mention that person's name. Mention that you're conducting a career change or, if you're a new grad, that you're researching career options. Ask for no more than 20 minutes of their time to discuss their career, the company and other questions you have about job opportunities in their field and industry.

3. Prepare yourself

Put together a list of questions to ask during the interview. Examples:

Job Related:
- What are your job duties?

- How did you get into this type of work?
- What is your background?
- What is the salary range for this occupation?
- What do you like and dislike most about your job?
- What advancement opportunities are there for this position?
- What qualifications are required for your position?
- What are the qualifications for an entry-level job in this career field?
- What personality traits are most important for your job?

Company and Industry-Related:
- How would you describe your company's culture?
- Who are your company's major competitors?
- What are the major trends projected for your industry over the next five years?
- What types of job opportunities does your company have?

Field Related:
- What professional organizations do you belong to or recommend that I join?
- What journals, books or articles do you recommend that I read about your industry or field?
- What professional conferences or seminars would you recommend that I attend for education and networking purposes?
- What other organizations or companies might be interested in someone with my background?

Additional Questions:
- Would you please give me feedback on my résumé? What works, doesn't work?

- Any suggestions about how I could market myself for opportunities in your career field?
- May I have the names of people that I can continue my career exploration discussions with?
- Do I have your permission to use your name as a referral?

Follow Up on Every Informational Interview

Ask for a business card when you meet, and always follow up with a handwritten thank-you note. Use the information from the business card to address the envelope. A handwritten thank you note demonstrates good manners and thoughtfulness. The thank-you note is a great marketing tool in itself because it sets you apart from most other people, who don't bother to follow up at all. Include your business card, if you have one. If not, be sure to write your phone number, e-mail address and home address on the bottom of the card. Who knows? You could get a call, if the person hears about a job lead.

The *Only* Five "Must-Answer" Job Interview Questions

Hate job interviews? Join the crowd. Interviewing today can be a gut-wrenching process, largely because you feel as if you are facing the *Inquisition*.

This is the major reason: Designed to scare every job seeker to death, websites and books on job interviews promote endless lists of "trick" job interview questions you absolutely MUST have answers for.

Your fear is that if you don't memorize the "correct" answer to each one, you'll probably blow the interview.

Good news: Throw most of those job interview questions in the trash! Here's why: These authors and so-called "experts" don't want you to know the truth, which is that an interview is just an opportunity for a company to get the answers to *five simple interview questions*.

Although they may seem simple on the surface, it's imperative that you have compelling answers for each one to allay their concerns. Here's the kicker: If you don't or can't answer any one of these questions to their satisfaction, you will not be hired or brought back for a future interview.

Here they are:

1. *"WHY ARE YOU HERE?"*

Before you walk into any interview or participate in any phone screen, you absolutely *must* learn something about the company. Do your research. Check out the company's website, especially their PR or Recent News section, where you'll find interesting info on your target.

They want to be flattered that you picked their company to interview. So tell them what you like or what impresses you about this company.

> **Bonus Tip**
>
> **Do your company research before you call. Work this into the conversation. Use your knowledge to ask an open-ended question such as:** *"I understand your company has recently introduced a more powerful widget. How has that worked out so far?"* **or** *"From the research I've done on your company, I see that you are getting into some new markets."* **(Be specific here, elaborate on the actual information you've uncovered).** *"That can be challenging. How is that working out so far?"* **These small tidbits are important, because it shows you're serious and that you've done your homework—and people always like talking about their own business successes.**

2. "WHAT CAN YOU DO FOR US?"

On the surface, this seems pretty simple. The job requires certain skills that you either do or don't have. Just because you have the skills, don't think you're done. This company is probably interviewing at least 20 other candidates who have the same skill sets as you. Why would they choose or even remember YOU when the day is done? Here's how: Give them your USP. That's the "Unique Selling Proposition" you developed earlier in this book. Sometimes called the "Value Added Proposition," this is a short sentence that sums up who you are and what benefit you bring to the company. Think of this as your "elevator pitch."

Long after the interview, your USP is what they remember.

3. "WILL YOU FIT IN?"

The alternative question is, "Can you be managed?" They already have a process and a team. They want to know how you'll fit with that team. They also want to know whether you can be managed. No company wants to hire a maverick, loner or prima donna.

So let them know that you're a team player. Do this by developing a few stories from your past work experience. Describe a successful project or team you've been a part of, the goal that was met and your role in that team's success. In fact, many of your answers should be couched in terms like "my company," "our team," and "our role."

4. "WHAT MAKES YOU UNIQUE?"

In a nutshell, they want to know whether you'll go that extra mile for them. And here's a great way to do that - tell them some "stories." These are short, personal narratives that you can share, taking no more than 30 to 90 seconds each. Start by developing your stories around areas such as:

- Instances when you either made money or saved money or time for your previous company.
- A crisis in your life or job and how you responded or recovered from it.
- A time when you functioned as part of a team and some unique contribution as a result.
- A time in your career when you had to deal with stress and what the outcome was.
- A time in your job when you provided successful leadership or a sense of direction.

You provide "stories" as answers to questions because they are unique and memorable and make you stand out over other candidates. They also make the interview more of a conversation and less of a Q&A interrogation. They also take the onus off memorizing answers to all those job interview questions.

5. "HOW MUCH WILL YOU COST US?"

Generally, salary doesn't come up in the initial interview. While there are ways of specifically handling this, don't get into a discussion about salary here. You need only to demonstrate a willingness to work with them within the confines of their compensation structure at this point. Keep it general. If they really want you, they'll find a way to pay you what you're worth at closing.

Knowing the five "must-answer" questions gives you a very big advantage over most of your competitors. It's imperative that you spend time now to develop your answers to each one of them. A great strategy in answering several of these questions is to use a technique called "telling your stories." That's the subject of the next chapter.

Tell Your Stories at the Interview

Many years ago, when I (Joe) hated what I was doing for a living, I was encouraged by my career coach to write down several short stories about times and events in my life when I influenced the outcome.

I was stumped at first, but after a few days I came up with over 15 pages of stories of times in my life when I significantly affected things in a positive way and either grew myself or bettered my lot or that of others around me.

So what does this have to do with a job interview?

If you read other books on job interviews, you'll notice they feed you lists of interview questions to which you must prepare answers. That's an old 'interrogation' paradigm that puts you, the job hunter, on an unequal footing with your interviewer. You essentially play the role of 'child' to an 'adult' interviewer who has all of the advantage.

Instead, as we pointed out when we talked about active and passive pursuit of employment, we want to move away from the idea that an interview is an interrogation and turn it into more of a conversation.

To accomplish this, you will need to come armed with a selection of small stories about both your business and personal life. These are short, 30- to 90-second narratives that describe an event in your past when you played a pivotal role. This "storytelling" concept is especially applicable for the competency-based type of interview that's common today.

In a traditional interview, the questions will be focused on whether you have the skills and knowledge needed to do the job. A competency-based interview goes further by asking you additional questions about your character and personal attributes; the objective for the interviewer is to be able to better determine whether you fit into the corporate culture. Broadly, these traits are called "behavioral competencies."

A competency-based interviewer will spend about half of the interview focusing on your job skills, and about half on your behavioral competencies. The interviewer will be looking for evidence of how you have acted in real situations in the past.

Having your stories ready in advance plays very well for this type of interview. A company wants to find out:

1. Are you an asset or liability? Will you either make money or save money for the company?
2. Are you a team player? Will you fit into the corporate hierarchy or act like sand in the gears? Can you take and, if appropriate, give orders?
3. Will you fit into the company culture? Employers don't want prima donnas. They want employees who can quickly understand the corporate landscape and fit in with their system and culture.

We want to emphasize again that an interview should not be an interrogation. It should be a conversation between two equals. When you accomplish this you are a big step closer to your goal of landing the job you really want, because it's the *conversation* that wins an interview, and it's the conversation that wins the *job!*

To facilitate the conversation and to keep it moving in your favor, have your stories ready. This simple advance preparation will make you stand out and be remembered positively when you are being compared to the other job applicants.

By combining your USP and your own easily remembered "stories," you won't be pinning your hopes on trying to memorize a "correct" answer to some "trick" interview question. Your stories are unique to your own experience, so you'll inevitably have a greater chance of leaving the interview room having made a positive impact and you'll stand a better chance of being considered for this particular job.

Next, we'll talk about developing a short list of questions YOU need to ask.

> **Bonus Tip**
>
> **Keep yourself on an equal footing with your contact. You do that by asking questions after every answer you give. Think of this as giving something and then getting something back in return. This is what a conversation is. Your objective is to get an interview, get another phone conversation, or get a lead. Stay focused and on track. Ask questions until you get at least one of the three objectives.**

Your Turn:
Six Questions You Must *Ask*
In Your Interview

We've talked about questions you need to have great answers for. Now it's your turn to take more command at your next interview by asking some pointed questions of your own.

Here are six "Must Ask" questions, plus the reasons you need to know the answers:

1. **"What happened to the last person who held this job?" (or, if a new position, "How has this job been performed in the past?")**

    Why you must ask this: You need to know any problems or past history that might be associated with this position. For instance, was the predecessor fired or promoted? Is this a temporary or a brand new position? Regardless of the answer, this will tell you about management's expectations and the growth areas this company is gearing toward.

2. **"Why did *you* choose to work here?"**

    Why you must ask this: Although you may like this company, you're an outsider. Find out what an insider has to say about working there. Who better to ask than your interviewer? This also forces the interviewer to step out of the official corporate role and answer personally as an employee and potential co-worker.

3. **"What is the first problem that needs the attention of the person you hire?"**

    Why you must ask this: You need to be on the same page as your new manager. You want to have a clear indication of the initial expectations and whether you can deliver same. You don't want to allow yourself to be mislead and end up overwhelmed and over your head after the first week on the job.

4. **"What can you tell me about the individual to whom I would report?"**

    Why you must ask this: It doesn't matter how wonderful the company might be, your time will be spent working for a specific manager. You need to find out about this person and his or her management style. If you're an independent type of employee used to working through solutions on your own, you'll chafe when you find you're being supervised by a micro-manager. Find out early so you can make adjustments before personality clashes might develop, or perhaps this job just isn't right for you.

5. **"What are the company's five-year financial projections?"**

    Why you must ask this: You need to know about the future of the company. It doesn't have to be this exact question. For example, you might want to ask about the company's future plans for new products and services or any market expansions in the works. Of course, you've done your own research, but nothing can beat the observations and insights of an insider. This also shows you've been doing your homework and you're serious about this company.

6. **"What's our next step?"**

    Why you must ask this: This is the 'closing' and the most important question you ask at the end of the interview. You need to know what happens after this point.

Many books advise asking for the job here, but you may feel intimidated to bluntly do so. With more candidates already scheduled for interviews, they're not likely to make you an offer yet.

You may also need to do some additional research on the company, making it too early to ask for the job.

A good compromise would be to take the lead and set a plan for follow-up. You'll also get a gauge of the hiring manager's enthusiasm when you get an answer.

Don't forget to ask for their direct phone number and the best time to call.

Put It on Paper

One final strategy to implement while you're getting answers to these questions is to *write down your answers*. There are several reasons for doing this:

- It shows you're really interested
- It puts you on a more equal footing
- It allows you to slow the pace down a bit
- It puts your interviewer on notice that what he or she says is "on the record," resulting in more truthful answers

As a job hunter, you know that the key to a good interview is to find out as much about your potential employer as possible. The questions you ask could prove every bit as important as those you answer. With these six simple questions, you will not only appear more committed as a candidate, you also will get better insight into both the challenges and the opportunities that may lie ahead for you.

Next up are answering strategies to three crucial questions almost every interviewer faces.

How to Answer
The <u>Other</u> Interview Questions

I said earlier that there are only five questions you *must* answer in any interview.

Here are three more specific questions you'll almost certainly get, and we'll look at how you can deal with each of them while simultaneously making a strong, positive impression on your interviewer.

Let's start here:

You walk into the interview room, shake hands with your interviewer and sit down with your best smile on. Guess what their first question is?

"Tell me about yourself."

Do you "wing it" and actually tell all manner of things about yourself? Will you spend the next five minutes rambling on about what an easy-going, loyal, dedicated, hard working employee you've been? If this is what you do, you will stand a good chance of boring your interviewer and creating a distinctly negative first impression.

Because it's such a common interview question, it strikes us as strange, indeed, that so few candidates spend the time to prepare a considered response. Perhaps because it seems so disarming and informal, we drop our guard and shift into "ramble" mode.

Resist all temptation to do so! Your interviewer is not looking for a ten-minute dissertation here. Instead, offer a razor sharp sentence or two that sets the stage for further discussion and sets you apart from your competitors.

Give them a "synopsis about you" answer, starting with the *Unique Selling Proposition* you've developed that is most relevant to the job you're interviewing for.

Here is an example from an interview for a retail management slot:

> "I'm a seasoned Retail Manager, strong in developing the kinds of training programs and loss prevention techniques that have resulted in revenue savings of over 2.3 million dollars for (current employer's name) during the past 11 years."

What a difference you've made with this statement! Your interviewer is now sitting forward in her chair and is giving you her full attention. At this point, you might add the following sentence:

> "I'd like to discuss how I might be able to do something like that for you."

The ball is now back in her court, and you've created the beginnings of a real discussion rather than an interrogation process. The key is that you must *lead with your strongest benefit to the employer*. Be specific and don't wander about with some laundry list of skills or talents. Be sure to put a monetary value on your work, if at all possible, and be ready with details when you're asked.

When you walk into an interview, always expect the "tell me about yourself" question. The advantages of this approach are that you'll quickly gain the interviewer's attention and interest them in knowing more, all the time keeping focus on the *employer's needs* rather than *your wants*. You'll separate yourself from your competitors. You'll also improve your chances of being positively remembered—and hired.

"Why do you want to work here?"

How you answer *this* question, which you'll almost always be asked during an interview, may well determine whether you receive a job offer. Here's how to separate yourself from the pack

Like the "tell me about yourself" question, this one, too, appears to be a simple inquiry, but if you want to put yourself a giant leap ahead of other candidates, be prepared to answer with information that will instantly convince the interviewer that you have given some real thought to your own future and your possible involvement with the company.

We'll assume that you've done your homework and researched the company—and that you reviewed your research before showing up for the interview. You're familiar with the firm's competitors, its industry position, its products (including their relative strengths and weaknesses in their industry), annual revenues (if available and relevant to the job you're seeking), the number of employees, locations of other offices, its history, culture, and so forth.

By the way, you don't have to memorize dozens or hundreds of facts and figures. Make good notes in advance on one or two three-inch by five-inch cards, and be willing to pull them out of your pocket or briefcase, refer to them, and give accurate information

(*Hint: on this little note sheet you can actually write out your answers and not have to remember anything at all!*).

This attention to detail and your apparent depth of interest will most assuredly flatter the hiring manager and impress him or her with your knowledge of the positives about the company.

More on this question: clarify the issue for yourself. There is another reason to prepare a strong argument for why you want to work for this company—and this one is about you. You must understand for yourself "Why do *I* want to work here?" Sometimes assertiveness and just "wanting the job more than the other guys" will trump even experience and historical qualifications.

Yes, it's not uncommon for less qualified candidates to be hired from a large pool of more experienced and skilled candidates. How can this happen? If asked, an employer often will respond with, "I hired her because she was more assertive and wanted the job more than the other more skilled applicants."

"What do you see as your biggest weakness?"

Interviews are not all about how wonderful you are. Every interviewer will be looking for a candidate's weaknesses as well as strengths, yours included. It's their job. After all, none of us is perfect.

Knowing this, you have an opportunity to position or "frame" your weaknesses to your best advantage. You will want to literally hand them a couple of weaknesses that can satisfy their quest and maybe limit further probing.

A good strategy is to prepare two weaknesses, one business-related and another one personal. They should be honest and believable but not be deal-breakers. You should also try to end each one with a positive spin, such as explaining how the weaknesses could be transformed into strengths in the new employer's company.

Suggested action step around the weakness question

Well before you enter an interview room, do this exercise:

List your *two* biggest weaknesses, *one personal and one business-related*. Then write out at least one positive result that has arisen or could arise from each weakness. Your goal, of course, is to demonstrate that you are aware of the problems and are compensating for them.

> Example:
>
> (Personal) *"I'm a real night owl because I like to read a lot. This can sometimes pose a little conflict when I'm around 'morning people' who like to rise at 4 a.m. I have to really work on my 'cheerfulness factor' early in the morning. I get a chance to read some great books, though. For instance, I just finished reading the book,* Blink, *by Malcolm Gladwell."*

Using the example above, write down your biggest **personal weakness.**

What did you do—or are you doing—to correct or counteract it?

Now think about your biggest business weakness while reading the following example.

> *"Even though I have really strong C++ programming skills, I lost out on a good project assignment because my scripting skills in Perl were weak. Since then, I have taken a course in Perl programming to enhance my skill level in this area. Although losing the assignment was not pleasant, it gave me a good near term goal to improve my skills."*

Now jot down your biggest **business** weakness.

Paycheck 911

What have you done—or are you doing—to correct or counteract it?

———————————————————————

OK. Now you're ready to score points while others fall by the wayside!

Job Search is a Sales Process

Remember that you are in a sales process and that buyers, whether they're buying a car or hiring an employee, buy for emotional reasons. They may or may not be consciously aware of this fact, yet your ability to appeal to their emotional needs can put you in a winning position during any part of the hiring process. After all, a decision to buy is based on an emotional need and is backed up by logic related to the employer's perception of which candidate has the best skills, personality, and so forth.

What, you may ask, are their emotional needs? These could include the following:

- To make the right hiring decision from a possibly overwhelming number of candidates
- To succeed as a hiring manager
- To find someone that brings positive energy and enthusiasm to the company, department or group
- To be liked . . .

. . . and that's only a partial list. There are countless emotional needs that can be satisfied by hiring the right person. Positive energy and enthusiasm are contagious. Use the answer to *"Why do you want to work here?"* as a strategy to win over the employer and to address at least some of these emotional needs.

The Ten Biggest Interview Killers

When you're on a romantic dinner date, you try to avoid "mood killers"—talking with a mouth full of food, cursing an ex-lover, or complaining about a foot ailment.

During a job interview, you have to avoid similar spoilers if you want to make a good impression.

Here are ten of the most common "advantage killers" and how you can avoid them during your next job interview:

1. *Not knowing your aim.* Too often candidates think their purpose in an interview is simply to ask for a job. Your goals are to demonstrate how you are a good fit for the organization, and to assess whether the job is really right for you.
2. *Being too needy.* Neediness is probably the No. 1 advantage-killer in an interview. Remind yourself before walking in the door: you do not need this job. You do need food, air and water. Keep things in perspective.
3. *Unconvincing nonverbal communication.* This is about demonstrating confidence. Your first impression makes the difference. When you enter the interview room, stand up straight, make eye contact, and offer a strong handshake with your interviewer. If necessary, jot their name on your notepad as soon as you seat yourself. Do the same for any other individual you are meeting with.
4. *Compromising your position.* You should always participate in the interview as an equal, not in the role of subordinate to the interviewer. Frequently, this is a subtle matter of self-perception, so remind yourself before the interview.
5. *Falling into the answers-only rut.* An interview is a conversation. Don't just answer their questions. That's why you've prepared stories to highlight your accomplishments, which will be your moments to shine. When you do answer questions, make sure that you answer immediately and follow up with a question of your own, if at all possible.
6. *Rambling.* Telling your interviewer more than they need to know could be fatal. Your stories should be 60 to 90 seconds long and have a relevant point. Focus, focus, focus. Stick with your rehearsed stories, your research, and the questions you need to ask. Don't fill up the silence with unnecessary talk.
7. *Being overly familiar.* A good interviewer will be skilled enough to put you at ease within the first ten minutes of the

interview. That doesn't mean that they have become your best friend. Don't let your guard down. You're there to interview them and get answers to your questions. Treat this from start to finish as the professional business meeting that it is.

8. *Making incorrect assumptions.* Points are not deducted for asking questions when you don't understand something. Don't guess at what your interviewer means. Effective interviewing is all about collecting information in real time, taking good notes, and responding only to the actual facts you've collected. If you find yourself making assumptions or guessing about something that was said, stop and ask for clarification before you answer.

9. *Getting emotional.* At times the interviewer may hit a nerve or consciously try to provoke you into an outburst. Don't fall for it. Clear your mind of any fears or expectations, so you can maintain a calm, open-minded perspective at all times. When emotions enter into an interview, failure follows.

10. *Not asking specific questions.* You want to find out more about what this job is really about and whether you want it. Arrive with a list of several prepared questions about the company, position and people who work there. Ask questions that begin with "What . . .?", "How . . .?", and "Why . . .?" Avoid simple yes/no questions. Get your interviewer talking as much as possible, and then take notes. Most interviewers are unimpressed by someone who has no questions—and impressed by interviewees who take notes.

Post-Interview

I may have said this before, but I can't stress it enough. To win the job you really want today, you need to stand out from all of your competitors. You need to do things other candidates don't do.

Remember, *the last person to be interviewed is the one who usually gets the job.* That means, if you haven't received the job offer, your work is not over. You need to find a way to be called back for that last interview, if at all possible. Therefore, you must look for ways to keep your name and skills in front of the interviewer. You've traveled this far, don't let down now. Go that extra inch and it may mean all the difference in the world.

Follow up With a Simple Interview "Thank You" Letter

One of those "extra inches" means to *always write an interview thank you note* to all involved at this interview. This is exactly one of those actions that very few candidates ever bother to do. True, e-mail might be more immediate, but nothing separates you from the pack like *a handwritten note.*

So, get a box of *plain* "Thank You" cards or small notepaper with envelopes from your local drug, grocery or stationery store. Use this to write your note.

Don't procrastinate. The clock is ticking, so address the envelope, put a stamp on it and *get it into the mail within 24 hours.*

The reason for all this fuss is that an interview thank you letter is a "stand out" tool. To win the job you really want today, you need to stand out from all of your competitors. Your extra effort here can make all the difference.

Elements of a Good Interview Thank You Letter

I'm not talking "hearts and flowers" letters here. I'm talking about a note that's short and to the point. Actually, three or four sentences is perfect.

Here is what you must say (be sure to include the following elements—one sentence each is fine):

Sentence 1: Thank them for the interview.

Sentence 2: Let them know you're excited about the job, you want it and can do it.

Sentence 3: (Optional) If you know what the first project (or task, or challenge) will be, then briefly mention that as well.

Sentence 4: Thank them again.

Sign it.

Now, mail it.

Here are a few important details to keep in mind:

If there were any others who took part in the interview, be sure to mention their names as well. If you met with them separately or they took a major role in the interview, send them a separate note.

An interview thank-you letter is not just a formality. It is a marketing communication that provides one last opportunity to sell *you*, the product. Be polite and respectful, but by all means don't be bashful about:

    (a.) your enthusiasm

    (b.) a particular job-related strength you possess

    (c.) the message that you can do, and want this job.

If you haven't asked for the job in the interview, then ask for it now in the thank you letter. This will be your last chance to sell yourself.

By using this simple template for your interview follow-up, you'll stand out from your competitors. By doing just this one thing, you can very well make the difference between getting lost in the shuffle and getting either a job offer or a second interview!

Now, go for it!

Section VI --
SUPPORT AND RESOURCES

In this section we will consider a "different" way to look at the whole process of job search, and we'll give you a few additional resources to tap along the way.

Dealing Emotionally With Your Job Search

If you're in job search mode right now, we don't have to tell you how negative emotions soon creep in. These may include feeling isolated, left behind, thrown away and—that favorite of mine—feeling like my career is over and I'll never get a decent job again. Ever!

The Loneliness of the Job Search Process: Sue's Story

Now it's time to focus on the *emotional* side of job search. Job hunting has got to be one of the loneliest times in anyone's life. I've personally gone through three career changes, each lasting from one to several years. I've also changed jobs many times during my varied careers as a psychiatric social worker, vocational rehabilitation counselor, technical recruiter and writer.

As I look back on my many forays into job hunting, I realize now that I could have made it easier for myself and not suffered quite as much as I did.

The hardest part for me was that nagging feeling that I'd never find that next job that was right for me. I felt that I was wandering in the desert searching for a job oasis that was just a mirage. I had to keep telling myself, "There is a better job up ahead; I'm not making it up; my seemingly unrelenting search for my next job *will* have a happy ending."

It required patience, faith and hard work, but I always found my way. Yet I also felt profound loneliness because I would usually withdraw and try to go it alone. This tendency to go into "loner mode" was partly the result of being unemployed, a natural path to isolation.

Those of you who are between jobs can relate to this, I'm sure. When you have a job, you're part of a community. The workplace can be dysfunctional, but it's still a community of co-workers. You have colleagues and a place to go every day. In contrast, an unemployed job seeker can find walking to the mailbox to pick up the day's mail the highlight of your day.

I would encourage anyone who's conducting a job search to stay connected with other people, especially those who can relate to what you're going through. Years ago, when I was a social worker with just a couple of years' work experience, I moved to Portland, Oregon. We didn't know anyone in that city.

I joined the local chapter of the National Association of Social Workers and started a group for unemployed social workers. We met at my house once a week. The meetings provided us with the opportunity to commiserate about our collective unemployment. We networked and shared job leads and information about the local job market. We cheered each other's successes and encouraged each other to keep going. The result was that our group disbanded about six months later because we'd all secured employment. It was a great reason to terminate the group.

I would encourage those of you who are unemployed and find yourselves slogging through day after day of an arduous job search, to reach out. You're not alone. And you're not victims. You share this temporary affliction with plenty of other fellow job seekers. This is a great opportunity to empower yourselves. With the Internet, there are so many opportunities to join other career changers and job hunters. One example, though certainly not the only resource, is MeetUp®.

If you can't find a group to join, start one yourself. You can begin with just one other job hunter, and expand the group out from there. You can meet in person at a restaurant or coffee shop, or communicate over the Internet. Job search groups can create a truly synergistic process.

The Five Secrets of Winning Job Hunters

Completing a 26-mile marathon race shares some characteristics with a successful job search. There is one "winner" who crosses the finish line first, and there are the many who quit before they've completed the race. Finally, there are the rest of us who don't finish first, but are determined to complete the race nevertheless. For most of us, half the battle is finishing the race, regardless of where we place among the finishers.

The same goes for a job search. We are veterans of many career changes and job searches too numerous to count. For both of us, job hunting made flying during turbulence, nails dug into the arms of our seats, seem relaxing by comparison. Yet they were learning experiences; what some call "character builders." The good news is that after each episode of job-hunting, we became better at the game. We also noticed that job hunting always strengthened and prepared each of us for our next job. Looking both at our own growth plus that of other successful job seekers, it boils down to five characteristics.

1. Visualize

Marathon runners and other goal-directed athletes are great at visualization. They set a goal and see themselves achieving it. The same applies for your job search. Set a goal and see yourself achieving it. No matter how many setbacks you have, hold that vision of the job you want. Continue to hold it. Focus on the outcome you want, and not on how you're going to achieve it. Picture it in your mind. Be specific. What is your supervisor like? How about your co-workers? What is your workspace like? What is your workday like? How do you dress? What hours do you work? Including your right brain in the imagination and visualization process enhances the achievement of your goal.

2. Be Persistent

Just as in running a marathon, nothing worth having is ever easy to achieve. There is a lot of rejection in job search. Sometimes it seems as if you'll never get a "yes." Remember what good sales people already know. That winning a sale, a job, or any other goal is a numbers game. Commission sales people will tell you that every "no" is one step closer to a "yes." When you can see your process from a more objective viewpoint, knowing that you're one more rejection closer to a "yes", you'll be less inclined to take the "no's" personally, and less likely to get discouraged.

3. Replenish Yourself

The job search process, like a marathon race, can be an endurance test with a lot of disappointments and setbacks. It can also go on for weeks, months, and for some people, even a year or more. Top marathoners know that they have to nourish their bodies in order to prevail. You need to nourish your mind and spirit as well. If you're going to outlast this process and prevail, you have to take care of yourself. This means taking time to relax to take your mind off the challenges, frustrations and rejections. Work hard on your job search, then take time out to exercise and pursue activities that bring you joy and replenish you.

4. Inoculate Yourself Against Negative Messages

Succeeding at a job search is a mental process, and negative input from anywhere can poison your mental outlook and encourage fear, discouragement, anxiety, anger and other negative emotions. Associate with positive people and protect yourself from all types of negativity. A job search journey can be a big undertaking. You need all of the assets and advantages that you can possibly bring to the party. You can't afford to be exposed to the negativity of others. This includes friends, relatives and negative articles in newspapers and magazines as well as negative TV shows. Make a point of reading books and articles that motivate, encourage and inspire you. Avoid anything and anyone that doesn't fall into this category.

5. Meditate

This can be the most important secret, yet it can be very simple. Take some time every day to be still and to get away from the "white noise" of life. Whether you are a spiritual person or not, commit to some quiet time away from the noise of TV, radio and other distractions. Give yourself the gift of quietness to contemplate, calm down and center yourself. Even five minutes of quiet time can make a positive difference in your life. This is an opportunity to relax, focus, and renew yourself. It will ground you and make it easier to face and overcome the stresses of your job search journey ahead.

As with successful marathoners, job hunters have some secret tactics that make their success look easy to others. Winning the job search game has a mental component. Developing the above five winning secret tactics will enhance your chances of success, and make the process more pleasant and less stressful.

Dealing Financially With Your Job Search

Before developing any new job-hunt strategies, make sure you tie down these loose ends in the financial area. After all, you want to have your financial house in order as much as possible so you can focus your time and energies on the hunt.

Did You Lose Your Job?

If you were terminated or if you quit or were otherwise downsized, this section is for you. Otherwise, skip to the last subsection, *Tax Deductions for Job Search.*

Unemployment Insurance

First and foremost, apply for Unemployment Insurance (UI) with the Department of Economic Security or equivalent in your particular state. Do it *now!*

Unemployment Insurance benefits are paid from a fund accumulated from taxes paid by employers. Generally, you must meet certain requirements to be eligible. You must be able to work, be available for work, willing to accept suitable work, actively seeking full-time work, and be out of work through no fault of your own.

If you voluntarily quit your job, the burden of proof is on you to show that you quit *for a good cause.* If you are terminated or discharged, your employer must show that you were terminated for work-connected misconduct as specified in your state's UI Law.

In most states, you may file your weekly claim for benefits by telephone or over the Internet; the choice is yours.

Typically, the first time you file for Unemployment Insurance benefits, your first week of unemployment is a week during which you meet all eligibility requirements. This is called a "waiting week." The waiting week is not a payable week.

With most states, your benefit year ends 365 days after your initial filing. You may have up to 26 weeks of Unemployment Insurance benefit payments, depending on how much you earned in your base period.

Benefits per week may range from $60 to a maximum of $250 (check with your state's policies for an exact figure) calculated from your highest quarter base period earnings.

Outplacement Services

After you have applied for UI, ask about outplacement services that may be available to you from your former employer. These are companies specializing in assisting the displaced employees. Their fees are usually picked up by the employer and the services can range from a one-hour seminar on job hunting to a long term approach consisting of one-on-one counseling to assist you in finding a new job.

Severance Packages

If you've been let go or "downsized" you may be eligible for severance pay. A week's pay for every year you were employed has been the standard. Ask for more if you can, citing your past performance and, especially if the unemployment rate is high, cite numbers. Guilt often works. In any event, if you don't ask, you won't receive.

Separation Benefits

Find out about any benefits for which you may continue to be eligible. With healthcare coverage, you should be able to continue coverage under a COBRA plan. Under COBRA law you are entitled to extend your current coverage for a period of 90 days. There may also be a subsidized rate for which you will be eligible for up to a period of 18 months from your separation. After that, you will have to pay at a higher personal rate.

Ask about References

Find out what kind of reference your manager can give. Because of today's potential legal entanglements, many companies will only give dates of employment and nothing more to those who inquire.

Before leaving the company, try to get a written testimonial letter from your current boss, if you have been on good terms. Write the letter yourself, if necessary, and have him sign it. It need not appear on company stationery, since it is simply a testament to your character and not an official recommendation.

Budgeting

Begin now to learn to live on a budget. Your job search may take only a matter of weeks. If you have no job and no other source of income, savings and other resources have a way of dwindling quicker than you might think. Credit difficulties will stress you to the max, strain your personal relationships, crush your morale and possibly paralyze you emotionally, preventing you from taking necessary actions in your job search.

Financial pressures can stop you dead in your tracks, and a "problem" credit report can even keep you from being hired. Remember, when you sign on the dotted line of the job application, somewhere in fine print, there is a line included that gives the employer the right to run a credit check. A bad credit rating has the effect of ending your candidacy for a job with many companies, as it is an indication of how you handle fiscal responsibilities. They make the assumption that this is how you might perform as a future employee by acting irresponsibly, even stealing from the company.

Credit Counseling

Check out the services offered by nonprofit firms such as National Foundation for Credit Counseling. You can find their website at www.nfcc.org. This and other organizations provide free and/or low cost financial counseling and might provide answers for you regarding personal and family finances.

Debt Consolidation Loans

A consolidation loan is a single loan taken out to cover the cost of all of your current debts, thus consolidating them into one bill. Debt consolidation loans are often secured by real estate or other assets you already own, but they are also offered on an unsecured basis (usually at a somewhat higher interest rate).

The purpose of this type of loan is to consolidate debt from other, smaller loans such as retail store charge accounts, credit cards and smaller personal loans from banks or finance companies. The overall aims of debt consolidation are to reduce interest costs and to lower your monthly payment. By reducing the sum of all of these individual monthly payments into a single payment, the APR (annual percentage rate) on the interest you pay may be reduced considerably from the higher rates often charged by credit card issuers.

The term of the loan can be fixed, and the monthly payment can be lowered while still providing a payment schedule that assures that the principal balance will decrease each month rather than just meeting the minimum interest payment without reducing the amount owed.

A further word on secured loans: because your home is used as security, or collateral, the lender is taking a fairly low risk in lending you money, so interest rates for secured loans are lower than for unsecured loans, for which the lender requires no form of security in order to grant you the loan and is, therefore, taking more risk.

Another option, and probably less expensive, is to look at re-mortgaging your home, as this would provide you the lowest interest rate, probably a rate just a bit higher than your current mortgage rate. This could release cash that is tied up in the equity in your home and enable you to pay off all of your debts and still be left with working capital to use for current expenses during your job search.

Tax Deductions for Job Search

There are certain tax deductions you can claim for job search expenses. Check with your accountant or go online to IRS (http://www.irs.gov/publications/p17/ch30.html) to learn whether any expenses you incur are tax-deductible. Take notes on what you spend, keep all receipts, and maintain good records.

Generally, you *can* deduct certain expenses you incur while looking for a new job in your present occupation, even if you do not get a new job.

You *can* deduct employment and outplacement agency fees you pay in looking for a new job in your *present* occupation.

You *can* deduct amounts you spend for typing, printing, and mailing copies of a résumé to prospective employers, if you are looking for a new job in your present occupation.

If you travel to an area and, while there, you look for a new job in your present occupation, you may be able to deduct travel expenses to and from the area. You *can* deduct the travel expenses if the trip is primarily to look for a new job. The amount of time you spend on personal activity compared to the amount of time you spend looking for work is important in determining whether the trip is primarily personal or is primarily job search-focused. Even if you cannot deduct the travel expenses to and from an area, you *can* deduct the expenses of looking for a new job in your present occupation while in the area.

You may choose to use the standard mileage rate to figure your car expenses. The current standard mileage rate (2007 tax year) is:

48.5¢ cents per mile for business miles. You *cannot* deduct these expenses if:

- You are looking for a job in a new occupation
- There was a substantial break between the ending of your last job and the start of looking for a new one
- You are looking for a job for the first time

See www.irs.gov/publications for more information.

Unemployed and Desperately Seeking a Pay Check?

The global economy has forced change on all job seekers. It has decreased available jobs and increased competition for them. Those of you with college degrees have no doubt noticed that having one is no guarantee of employment, and it can be challenging, regardless of degree status, to find suitable employment.

Here are four job tips for successfully navigating the job search waters:

1. Get into the Game

If you're serious about finding employment, become proactive. Stretch yourself, get out of your comfort zone and aggressively seek out the hidden job market. This requires a game plan and the expectation that you're going to win this game. Using all the tools we've presented in this book, decide to excel and achieve at job search. Do something every day to further your search. Positive action diminishes anxiety and other negative feelings. This goes beyond survival of the fittest. For anyone who wants to succeed, it requires an iron will and determination that you will not be defeated by this job search process. You will prevail and you will outlast this challenge. Remind yourself of that.

2. Lose the Neediness

Take the words "desperate" and "defeat" out of your vocabulary. Employers can sense neediness and they won't hire you. If you present yourself with a sense of desperation, you're bringing your anxiety and fears to the table. Rather, focus on what you can do for an employer. Don't focus on *your* needs. Instead, focus on what the *employer* needs.

3. Think ROI

Employers don't hire people to be *liabilities* on their balance sheets. They hire people to be *assets* (provide a Return on their Investment). Employers hire you to solve a problem. To do this, demonstrate clear benefits that you offer them.

Take a look at your skills, experience, abilities and talents. Determine how you can best help the employer either make money or save money. Turn your skills and talents into benefits that an employer understands and appreciates. Pull out examples from your past work experience.

Ask yourself, *"How did my work save time or money, make money or otherwise improve the overall situation for my employer?"* An education and skill set, while valuable, do not translate into benefits. What can you do for this employer that your competitors can't? You have a unique set of skills, experiences and talents. Turn them into a "unique selling proposition" for the employer.

4. Think Outward

In the past, it was easier to get by with a traditional job search process; i.e., responding to ads found in the newspaper—or later, on the Internet. That was before the bar was raised. Now it's foolhardy to limit yourself to just responding to job ads on the Internet and expect success. Aggressively seek out those 80% of jobs not advertised.

Start widening your network both in person and online. Begin by making some new contacts each week through local events or related professional meetings. Online, you can add your bio to LinkedIn[R], Spoke[R] and even Facebook[R], for starters. Don't forget family, friends and neighbors who might know someone. Job searching is tough enough. Don't isolate yourself behind a computer screen.

When you apply the above tips, you no longer need to be "desperately seeking a paycheck." Instead, you will be "proactively seeking a match for your skills, experience, talents and abilities."

Sure, it'll be hard work at first. But over time your anxieties will lessen and you'll begin to see your prospects widen.

Dealing Spiritually With Your Job Search

The Secret became a phenomenal, best-selling success in early 2007. Its message is that we are all governed by the Law of Attraction, through which whatever we are holding in our mind and feeling is attracted to us.

"Like attracts like at a thought level," says Bob Doyle, author and Law of Attraction specialist, who also states in *The Secret*, "and so as you think a thought, you are also attracting *like* thoughts to you."

If you find yourself in one of the following categories, then you could greatly benefit from the principles of the Law of Attraction:

- You're looking for your first job.
- You've been laid off, downsized or fired.
- You're employed, but seeking a better job or career.

Regardless, now that you've gotten this far in our book you've got a new title: *Job Hunter.*

It's a safe bet that you're not thrilled with the prospect of job search. Who is? It's the equivalent of a root canal in the employment arena. The good news is that you don't have to do it alone. Harness the power of the Universe and apply the principles of the Law of Attraction to simplify and streamline your job search. Attract the right job for you now.

Apply the three principles of the Law of Attraction to:

- Feel more positive and energized about your job search.
- Shorten the time it takes to find a suitable job.
- Attract more positive people and better networking contacts.
- Attract opportunities that are a better match to your job goal.
- Land the right job for you.

Apply Three Winning Principles from **The Secret** *To Attract Your Next Job*

Principle #1 – Ask for What You Want

The first step in the creative process of manifesting what you want in life is simply to ask.

Lisa Nichols, co-author of *Chicken Soup for the African American Soul,* from the best-selling worldwide series, suggested in *The Secret* that when you make a command to the Universe, indicating exactly what you want, the Universe will respond to your thoughts.

Robert Collier, author of the self-help classic, *The Secret of the Ages*, described this important principle when he wrote, "See the things that you want as already yours. Know that they will come to you at need. Then let them come. Don't fret and worry about them. Don't think about your lack of them. Think of them as yours, as belonging to you, as already in your possession."

Get clear on what you want. If you send out a mixed message, you'll receive mixed results. Become as clear as a clean window about what you really want. This is powerful. Know that you can have, be or do anything. Know too, that there are no limits.

Action steps

Focus specifically on what you want. Picture your ideal job and see it in your mind.

Be clear and focused when you visualize the job.

- Write a description of your ideal job including job title, salary, benefits, duties, type of company, a description of your co-workers, what you'll wear to work, how you'll travel to and from work, even the job's approximate distance from home.

- Draw a picture of your ideal job because that engages your right brain as well.

- Hold the vision of that job, no matter what obstacles you encounter.

Include the phrase "this or better" when you think about your ideal job. Always leave the Universe the option to deliver the "right" job to you. It's important to acknowledge that you don't know which exact job is best for you.

Detach from a specific outcome. Holding a vision is powerful. Surrendering to the Universe by saying "this or better" is even more powerful.

Principle #2 – Believe It Will Happen

"Fear imprisons, faith liberates; fear paralyzes, faith empowers; fear disheartens, faith encourages; fear sickens, faith heals," wrote Harry Emerson Fosdick, Protestant minister, teacher and author.

According to *The Secret,* the second principle to successful manifestation using the Law of Attraction is to believe. This means you must, in the moment that you ask, believe and know you already have it in the unseen. When you believe and know that you have it in the unseen, a shift occurs in the entire Universe to bring it into the seen.

Job search is ultimately a journey of faith. It is a time when you have to believe that something you want is up ahead, even when you can't see it.

Everything that you are and have in your life now is the result of the Law of Attraction, a universal law that governs all of us. The Law of Attraction determines what you bring into your life. If you focus on negative feelings such as fear, you will attract circumstances and people that are also fear-based.

Action steps

Act, speak and think as though you are receiving it right *now*. The Universe is a huge mirror through which the Law of Attraction actually mirrors back to you your dominant thoughts. When your dominant thoughts contain the recognition that you don't have something, you continue to attract "not having it."

Believe that you already have it and have already received it.

Principle #3 – Receive

The third principle of the Law of Attraction is receiving. Surprisingly, this can be tricky. According to Nichols, receiving involves beginning to feel wonderful about the subject of your manifestation. She suggests that you emit the feeling frequency of having already received it.

Action steps

Feel that feeling *now* about the job you want. Feel as if you have it right now. What does it feel like working at your new job? How do you feel about your co-workers? What do your surroundings feel like to you? How do you feel about your boss? How do you feel about your workday? Are you having fun? Does the day whiz by quickly? Start to feel these aspects of your new job. Put yourself there and begin to *feel* the experience. In *The Secret,* Marci Shimoff, co-author of *Chicken Soup for the Woman's Soul* and *Chicken Soup for the Mother's Soul,* adds that it's important to feel good and to be happy. Feeling good puts you in the frequency of what you want to manifest.

"It's important to both believe and feel in order to have enough power to manifest whatever it is that you want in your life," says Michael Bernard Beckwith, founder of Agape International Spiritual Center, another *Secret* contributor.

Is there a fast track to get onto that frequency? According to Beckwith, it's necessary to do the following: say to yourself, "I am receiving now. I am receiving all the good in my life, now. I am *(fill in your desire)* now."

He adds you must feel it as though you have already received it.

Summary

You can conduct your job search alone, which is the hard way, or you can conduct it by harnessing the power of the Universe through applying the principles of the Law of Attraction.

For more details on how to apply these principles in your life, refer to *The Secret* by Rhonda Byrne.

Consciousness, Gratitude, and Living in the "Now"

Especially while we are job hunting, it's important to be conscious and aware of the good in our lives and feel appreciation despite outer circumstances or conditions. Our happiness isn't about how much stuff we've accumulated. Rather, it's about feeling grateful for who, what and where we are *right now*. It's about gratitude for how far we've come, what we do and for the challenges we've worked through.

Gratitude is critical to the success of our job search. According to author Rhonda Byrne, we attract what we think about and concentrate on through the universal Law of Attraction. When we focus on our cup being half full, we attract more abundance and prosperity. This includes job opportunities.

Conversely, when we think that job hunting is hard, and if we focus on the jobs we didn't get offered, we attract more rejection and disappointment.

It's been said that "Attitude is everything." That's especially true in job search. Although we may not control anything outside of ourselves, we are in control of what we think, feel and do.

Why not try these four simple gratitude steps to improve your job search?

1. Start a Gratitude Journal

Oprah Winfrey has credited her success in part to keeping a gratitude journal, logging in at least five items each night for which she's grateful. This shifts your energy. "What we think about and thank about, we bring about", according to Dr. John Demartini, *The Secret*. Adopt an "attitude of gratitude" and start writing down five items each day for which you are grateful. This gets easier after a few days and soon it starts to shift your mindset from lack to prosperity.

2. Focus on prosperity

Jack Canfield, co-author of the book series, *Chicken Soup for the Soul,* suggests focusing on prosperity and abundance. Focus on inner joy, peace, vision, and the outer things appear naturally. "Your voice and vision on the inside", he adds, "must be louder than the noise outside."

3. Visualize without limits

Joe Vitale, also featured in *The Secret,* suggests that you close your eyes in the morning and visualize what you want without limits. Then focus on what you're grateful for. He mentally reviews a gratitude list in the shower. He then releases all of this to the Universe, while breathing deeply.

Jack Canfield adds, "Energy flows where attention goes."

4. Be grateful – even when a job falls through

When you pursue job opportunities, always leave the Universe the option to deliver the "right" job to you. It's important to acknowledge that you don't know which exact job is best for you.

Be grateful, even when a certain job opportunity falls through, and always detach from a specific outcome. When job opportunities fall apart, it's probably true that the job wasn't right for you. Who knows why? No matter. Surrender to the Universe, knowing that the best job *for you*, will come to you at the right time.

The Wisdom of It All

The wise give thanks for what most of us take for granted. Spend a few quiet moments to try some of these simple, yet powerful steps. These steps, based on gratitude and the Law of Attraction, will help move you toward the right job for you at the right time.

Additional Resources

Additional Resources for Further Reading

Job Search and Career Change

Bolles, Richard N., *What Color is Your Parachute?* Berkeley, California: Ten Speed Press, 2005.

Spiritual Resources

Abrams, Dr. Michael, *The Twelve Conditions of a Miracle, The Miracle Worker's Handbook*, Boulder, Colorado: Abundance Media, 2001.

Byrne, Rhonda, *The Secret*, Hillsboro, OR: Beyond Words Publishing, 2006.

Chopra, Deepak, *The Seven Spiritual Laws of Success: A Practical Guide to the Fulfillment of Your Dreams*, San Rafael, California: Amber-Allen Publishing, 1994.

Dyer, Dr. Wayne W., *The Power of Intention: Learning to Co-create Your World Your Way*, Carlsbad, California: Hay House, Inc., 2004.

Gaines, Edwene, *The Four Spiritual Laws of Prosperity, A Simple Guide to Unlimited Abundance*, Holtzbrinck Publishers, 2005.

Hicks, Esther and Jerry, *The Law of Attraction, The Basics of the Teachings of Abraham,* San Antonio, Texas: Abraham-Hicks Publications, 2006.

Ruiz, Don Miguel, *The Four Agreements,* San Rafael, California: Amber-Allen Publishing, Inc., 1997.

Tipping, Colin C., *Radical Forgiveness, Making Room for the Miracle,* Marietta, Georgia: Global 13 Publications, Inc., 2002.

Tolle, Eckhart, *The Power of Now, A Guide to Spiritual Enlightenment,* Vancouver, B.C.: Namaste Publishing, 1999.

Williamson, Marianne, *A Return to Love, Reflections on the Principles of A Course in Miracles,* New York, N.Y.: HarperCollins Publishers, Inc., 1993.

Zukav, Gary, *The Seat of the Soul,* New York, N.Y.: Simon and Schuster, Inc., 1989.

About the Authors

Joe's Story

Known on the Internet as *"The Job Search Guy,"* Joe Turner built a winning job search system that he's taught to thousands of job seekers worldwide with his first book, *Job Search Secrets Unlocked!* Joe followed up with *Job Search Guy's Interview Prep Workbook* to answer growing demands for a straightforward no-nonsense approach to job interview preparation. As a recruiter, Joe spent 15 years finding and placing top candidates in some of the best jobs of their careers. He shares insights about today's job search scene on his blog, www.jobsearchguy.com. He's also been interviewed on radio talk shows and offers free insider job search secrets at: www.jobchangesecrets.com. Joe received a B.A. degree from the University of California at Berkeley and resides in Phoenix, Arizona, with his wife, Sue Swenson.

Sue's Story

An entrepreneur by nature, Sue grew a thriving business as a recruiter serving the semiconductor industry. Sues' previous careers include drug and alcohol counselor and rehabilitation counselor. Now a writer, she offers her job search and recruiting expertise by contributing regular blog articles and co-writing books with Joe Turner. As the economy worsens and companies face major layoffs, the market requires a new, effective approach to job search. Joe and Sue address this compelling need with the launch of this new book, *Paycheck 911: Don't Panic! Power Your Job Search.* Sue holds a B.A. degree from the University of Wisconsin, Madison, and a Masters degree from Michigan State University. Married to Joe Turner, Sue resides in Phoenix, AZ.

Your resume is your #1 marketing tool.
Is it selling you effectively?
Are you winning interviews?

As a purchaser of *Paycheck 911*, I'm offering you a personal no-charge consultation to determine how well your résumé is selling you. Discover important changes you can make to create a résumé that opens doors for you.

Communicate directly with the "Job Search Guy" to determine how to build a more effective résumé for today's tougher job market.

E-mail your résumé to info@job444.com and include *"Paycheck 911 Résumé Evaluation"* in the subject line.

We'll schedule a convenient time to talk by phone to move you one step closer to building a "Killer Résumé" that effectively sells you for the job you really want.

For those who are outside of the US and Canada, we'll communicate by e-mail.

Printed in the United States
221921BV00003B/2/P